7

WHERE LAND MEETS SEA

WHERE

LAND MEETS SEA

The Enduring Cape Cod

written and engraved by CLARE LEIGHTON

David R. Godine, Publisher, Inc., Boston

This is a Nonpareil Book published in 1984 by
David R. Godine, Publisher, Inc.
306 Dartmouth Street, Boston, Massachusetts 02116

Library of Congress Cataloging in Publication Data

Leighton, Clare, 1899–
Where land meets sea.
(A Nonpareil book; 32)
Reprint. Originally published: New York:
Rinehart, 1954.
1. Cape Cod (Mass.) — Addresses, essays, lectures.
I. Title. II. Series.
F72.C3L4 1984   974.4'92   81-20080
ISBN 0-87923-424-5   AACR 2

First printing

Printed in the United States of America

Contents

WHERE LAND MEETS SEA

Foreword

"But there are so many books about Cape Cod," a friend said, as I admitted to writing this. "Far too many of them, I should say. How can there be need for another?"

My defense is that I do not really consider this a book about Cape Cod. It is merely a gathering together of my own personal impressions. There is nothing authoritative about it, and it would be a failure as a guidebook. I give no information, and history is something I have left untouched. How else could that be, when I remind my readers that I was a Britisher by birth and am a Cape Codder of only ten years' standing?

I have written this book solely because I wanted to do so. And I wanted to do so because I happen to love the Cape deeply.

It is normal to want to write or sing about something you love. Love is the stimulus that has created some of the finest of our ballads and songs; it is an emotion that can illumine a land just as glowingly as it can a man or a woman.

Because I love this particular earth and sea I have tried to show the basic, enduring life of Cape Cod. Too many of us come here only during the months of summer, when the scene is cluttered with vacationists, and the true spirit of the land is forced into hiding. There is great beauty here, in the summer; but it is the more obvious beauty that might, more or less, be found elsewhere. It remains for the hard, wind-buffeting months of winter to disclose the Cape in its greatest subtlety.

If I seem to have given emphasis to this season of gaunt grandeur, it is because I believe it to be too little known. It is not enough to lie on golden, sun-warmed sands, watching a satin-smooth blue ocean. The rhythm of the year, then, is only partially fulfilled. We must watch, as the beach grasses change their brilliant green to a dull ochre, and the samphire of the marshes flames into flamboyant orange. Cape Cod, then, in the fall of the year, is fantastic in its glory of color. It is aflame with extravagance.

But fully to love the Cape, we must live with the loneliness of winter, and be fearless against the assault of a northeaster. We must know it in the setting of wind and storms and implacable fog, and be willing to take months of damp gloom, when the bare gray trunks of the honey locust toss, as the wind whines and howls. Only then can we enjoy to the full those incomparable days of sun and sea that come in their due season.

But, above the rhythm of the year, of greater value is the life of the workers upon this land and sea. You know a country only insofar as you place your finger on the pulse of the workers within that country. If you would know and love Cape Cod you must be aware of the fishermen and their families.

In some strange manner, all these people vanish from sight over

4

the months of summer, suddenly to appear immediately after Labor Day. Then the Cape wakes from its stupor and shakes itself to a brisk, clean integrity.

Summer and winter, sunshine and storm; I have tried to give my impressions of these swings of the pendulum. For only thus can we get a full picture of Cape Cod.

And yet, I know, there is so much I have left unsaid—possibly particular things that my readers will want most to hear about. I have devoted myself almost entirely to the lower Cape, and especially to the neighborhood of Wellfleet, which is what I know best.

I would add that obviously this book is written by a woman. It is the book of an onlooker, a devoted onlooker but very often an ignorant one.

But above all I hope I have been able to instill into it something of the feeling of the universality of the sea, so that, though the setting may chance to be Cape Cod, yet it will belong to all sea and all shores, everywhere, and delight those who love a watery world —a tide line world, you might call it, where land meets sea.

Clare Leighton

Wellfleet, Cape Cod
Woodbury, Connecticut

Hurricanes
and Storms

It was just before Labor Day when the hurricane happened. I remember this, because all the summer people were still here. They had been watching for it over several days, listening to the reports on the radio. The vacationists must have spent a considerable time worrying about it, growing more and more tense as they heard it had passed Bermuda and was coming up the Florida coast. Then came the news that the airfields of North Carolina had been ordered to move their planes inland, and, a little later, that the Eastern Shore of Maryland and the coast of New Jersey had been alerted.

Of course, you did not know for sure that the hurricane would strike Cape Cod. It could change its course, as so many of them did, and veer out to sea. All the same, though, it was better to

7

be on the safe side. Terrible things had happened before now.

And so, that morning, you could have seen quite a procession of cars driving up the Cape, heading inland. The filling stations ran out of gas. Many summer cottages were hurriedly closed. It looked almost as though Labor Day had happened before it was due.

None of this would have taken place if it had not been for the radio. Neither would the storm have been dignified with the name of hurricane. Big blow, the Cape Codders would always have called it; squall, or gale, or even a breeze. And this was not because the storms in the past had been less intense, old Charlie Mayo assured me. It was merely that the radio knew how to make things sound important.

The fishermen were scarcely aware of this summer exodus. They were far too busy leading their own lives to bother their heads about such trifles. But neither did they trouble to listen to the radio. After all, why should you need to rely on it, when you could tell the weather yourself, by all the signs that fishermen have always known back across the ages? There was the particular way the morning sun came up, partly obscured and all brassy, with a yellowish tinge where ordinarily it was red. And the way the gulls acted—soaring way up in the sky with a high wind, while the air was flat calm all around. And suddenly, if you noticed it, the loons would leave the harbor and take refuge on the ponds; that was an unmistakeable token. And then, if you began to get a bit worried, all you had to do was to tap the glass of the barometer. You could always tell by the way the glass went down slowly and gradually, till the pressure got fantastically low, that something was about to happen.

Not that this meant there was anything to get in a panic about. All you had to do, if a gale were really coming, was to see that the boats were safe.

8

For the fishermen's boats are the tools of their livelihood. It doesn't matter too much if some of the shutters of the house are blown off, or even if the woodshed and the privy are overturned. The houses themselves have stood storms over a century, and you can trust they will go on standing them. But the boats are something very different.

Now, that particular morning Elisha Lamson had felt an apprehension about the weather. Not only had he noticed a funny, unusual light in the sky the evening before, but as the sun set, he had seen sundogs at the side of it. To bear this out, he was having trouble with his ears. They snapped and cracked and felt just as if he were high up in an airplane. He tapped the glass of his barometer and he didn't like what he saw. Other fishermen, all around, had done this identical thing, and had felt the same about it. It looked as though they were in for a breeze. Out at the Coast Guard station, on the back shore, the storm signals had been hoisted—those ominous squares of red with their black squares in the center, one flag above the other.

The day had started out in brilliant sunshine. The sky was exceptionally clear. If it were not for the fishermen's warnings and the news over the radio no one could have supposed that a tropical storm was on its way.

In spite of this beautiful weather, though, you could feel tension in the air, like a heated, tight-strung wire. How much of this tension was due to reactions to the reports over the radio and how much to the actual electricity in the atmosphere, it was hard to know. But there was no doubt about it, the gulls seemed agitated; they circled and mewed with unusual restlessness. Nerves were drawn taut, and you could see strain in the faces of the people you met, and hear it in their voices as they discussed plans for safety.

But the fishermen remained calm, as fishermen have always

done. They watched the wind, that they might know the best refuge for the boats.

"Where are you going to lay?" they asked each other. No longer were they individuals. They had become one, moving in a single body, concerning themselves only with the boats.

"If this wind is coming out of the southeast," they said, "we'd better make for Duck Creek."

Over the hours of the day they watched, their course of action waiting upon the quarter of the wind.

As the morning passed, you could see the fishermen quietly hauling the boats ashore, well up beyond the danger line. For, if the breeze hit, raising the water level and skimming the surface off the bay, it would churn the sea into cruel force, creating gigantic waves that could buffet the little craft against the wharf, or the beaches, or even against each other, till they got beaten as though they were of no greater strength than a few wooden matchsticks.

The draggers were taken around within Shirttail Point, far up into Duck Creek. And there they clumped together—*Two Sisters, Damned If I Know, Peter* and *Sue, Heart's Delight;* they were lashed together in groups of four, with old rubber tires between them, so that, should the big blow come, they would rise and dip upon the water as one, with increased resistance. Wherever possible, the boats were brought out of the water. Tony Elliot, who had worked all summer on his sloop, and loved it—though he was not a fisherman—with that special love of a man for his boat, grew scared, and sailed it, for safety, to the Cape Cod Canal. My neighbor's boys—young Peter and little Tommy—brought their skiffs to the shelter of the dunes, and hid them in the mud among the grasses along the shore of the cove. Down by the town beach, where at low tide the flats were dotted with dories, nothing was to be seen. The boats had been brought in. The harbor was deserted.

The brightness of early morning had changed. Sunshine gave way to haze, and a queer stickiness and oppression came into the air. The heavy, opaque atmosphere made it difficult to breathe. The sky now was gray, layered in curdled cloud, with no light of sun anywhere. Strange little eddies of wind broke into the stillness. Involuntarily, I found myself becoming charged with a sense of doom.

You could call it what you wished: hurricane, tropical storm, gale, big blow, white squall, or even breeze. No one could tell what it was going to be like when actually it arrived. I began to feel tense fear, of which I was ashamed.

I think it was the radio that made things worse. As I walked along the street the reports could be heard coming from every house. I was not allowed to forget it.

But then, just as I began to shrivel in my spirit through fear of the unknown, I met old Zenas Higgins.

He was wanting to talk to someone. Too old to help with the boats, he was feeling left out and alone. He needed to belong, and to satisfy a sense of drama and importance, as all men do when they face a possible catastrophe of nature's creation. So, now, with the threat of the wind uppermost in his mind, old Zenas was thinking back to other storms, in years gone by, before any of us were born.

"I'd been a coastguardman for over forty years before I got too old," he wheezed at me, scarcely able to stop his coughing. "Walked the beach, night after night, winter and summer, and sometimes, I tell you, that wind blew so strong that the oilskins I wore would be destroyed in just one day, with the blown sand cutting them. . . . Powerful thing, sand is, when it takes it into its head to blow like that. . . . And there was one night of a storm, when I was walking the beach—just near to the Highland Light—

and the telegraph wires were singing so loud, in the squall, even way up on the cliffs, you could hear them above the roar of the wind. And when they snapped—as they often did, in such a gale—when they snapped you could hear it for miles. I know storms, I can tell you. Lived against them for well over eighty years, and walked in them for forty."

Zenas Higgins drew his eighty-five-year-old body up straight and tall, recollecting dramas in which he had played his part as one of the chief actors.

The day passed. Those summer people who had remained listened still to the reported progress of the hurricane. The fishermen waited. They had secured their boats. There was nothing else that mattered. They had little fear of what might befall them. Trusting their land, and loving it, they knew it could not turn traitor to them. Possibly the beaches would be eroded, and big chunks might drop off the dunes. But this had happened over the centuries, and it could happen again. When it came to their houses, they still felt no concern.

And it was the quiet philosophy of the fishermen that made me realize the horribly destructive element of sustained fear. I began to wonder whether, in the balance of the human spirit, it was even good to know so far ahead—days and days ahead, over the radio —what *might* happen.

I found myself trapped between the anxiety of the summer people with their awareness of the world as a whole, its tornadoes, its tragedies, its violence, and the almost Biblical, trusting faith of the Cape Cod fishermen. And confusion overcame me.

Night fell at last. Already the heavens had opened, and the rain pelted down. It had fallen, thus, for many hours. Tension ran through the town, unifying us as nothing else could; for it is in times of possible danger that we surrender our separate entities

12

and become as one. Into our midst, to places of comparative safety, we gathered all those people from outlying, exposed areas—the artist and his wife from the high cliff overlooking the back shore, the family with four small children on the point of one of the heads of the bay, the little old woman who lived alone on the moors behind Truro. We brought them into the human warmth and companionship of the town, to houses that had withstood storms over more than a century.

I was even persuaded to go and try to bring old Mrs. Eldredge, the bedridden widow of a fisherman, to a place of greater safety.

And then, once more, this pendulum swung from fear to faith.

"Me?" shouted the aged widow from her bed by the window. "What? Me move, just because a wind might be coming along? What do you think of me? Me, who never stirred from this house in a storm—no, not even at the time of the Portland gale?"

And then I remembered something. This expression "the Portland gale" held magic for these people. It was something whereby they dated the events of their lives. A child had been born the week after the Portland gale. A husband had died a few months before the Portland gale. Old Aunt Bethia had been taken sick just a year after the Portland gale. I was tampering with something greater and more serious than I knew of. I was toying with the past—with memories of the day when the steamship *Portland* had been wrecked off Peaked Hill, that November of 1898, the day of the greatest storm in living memory. I, an outsider, a foreigner, was daring to suppose that a mere hurricane, possibly about to happen, could compete in fury and danger with this gale that had taken place before I had been born.

Humbled and apologetic, and yet braced in the spirit, I left the house of old Mrs. Eldredge. At this moment I feared nothing. I had met a human being who held the true kind of courage.

13

There was little sleep that night, among the off-Capers, though the radio had begun to reassure us. The course of the hurricane was still heading towards Cape Cod. But it was losing force.

Not a single fisherman, however, lost his sleep. Each one of them went to bed just as though it were an ordinary night, after an ordinary day. Probably they were not even aware of the tension around them. What they did know was that you cannot do anything about it when the elements kick up, so you might just as well get some rest and be ready for the things you will have to face next day. Their women, lying there beside them, may have felt less willing to sleep. In a trusting way, utterly devoid of panic, they would slip out of bed and go downstairs and read the Bible—just so as to keep right with the Lord. And, too, they had to be ready to wake their men at midnight, at the turn of the tide.

"Mind you wake me," said Elisha Lamson. "When the tide turns I want to go down for the last time, perhaps, and see how my boat is riding."

Over on Indian Neck the lawyer from Cleveland was awake. He had decided to brave the hurricane and had stayed. All the windows had been battened down. There was no sleep that night in his household. In common with the fishermen's families, they had drawn a supply of drinking water and trimmed the kerosene lamps. But fear stalked them, dwarfing the spirit.

Actually, when it finally came, it was not so dreadful after all. It might almost have been called an anticlimax. By the time the storm reached Cape Cod it had lost a large part of its violence. But even this depleted strength was enough to cause considerable havoc. Houses had rocked, and the heavens had emptied themselves in rain. We got up next morning—those who had been filled with fear rose from a sleepless night—to find the electricity was off. We crept around, wondering what had been happening.

14

Even the true Cape Codders could tell a dramatic story, once it was over and done with.

"It was like a mighty wind out of the Scriptures," said old Mrs. Sears.

"My house shook from the very earth beneath it," sighed Mrs. Mayo.

"And it was almost as if I could actually *see* the storm," added Gamaliel Newcomb. "Almost as if I saw the very blow itself. For I stayed up all the night long—seeing as I didn't have my boat any longer—and watched it out of the back window, knowing just exactly where it was coming from. And there, in the darkness, up against the dark, it was just as if I could see it, the wind blew so strong."

The wind still blew.

I drove to the back shore, to look at the ocean. The beach grasses were coated with wet sand; they leaned low with the weight of this sand. Everything in nature was limp, exhausted, spent.

The sea was white all over. It was still churning, curdled and wild from the storm. Spindrift misted the outlines of the breakers, giving them a transparent, almost gauzy appearance. The tide had brought the ocean to the foot of the dunes, and even half way up them—a seventeen-foot tide, it must have been, at the very least. Waves still raced up the side of those dunes, backing down in circular whorls of mighty force. They were buff in color, filled with the loosened sand. The storm had torn the sand from the dunes, exposing great stretches of dark brown clayey earth beneath.

I turned towards the wind, which was still violent. But I could not face that way. The sand, blown by this fierce wind, pricked and stung me. I felt I was being pierced by millions of red-hot needles. This, then, was what old Zenas had meant when he talked of the power of sand. And this that I was reluctant to face was what all coastguardmen had been exposed to and took for granted as they walked the beach in a storm.

When I returned to the car, I found that even the glass from my windshield had been pitted by the blast of the hurled sand.

The sun was shining; half of the sky was blue. But the light of the sun that morning seemed different. It was purged by the storm, a strangely cold, clear, white light, bleaching the sand and silvering the raging sea. And there, across the sea, like a great inverted bowl, was the vanishing hurricane. It was definite in shape, deep inky gray in color. It lay upon the horizon and arced in radiating bands of paler gray. It was violent of appearance, and very evil. Never had I supposed a hurricane could be so evident, something to which one could point in the sky and say: "There it goes, outward to sea."

After a while I managed to stumble down the dunes to the edge of this churning ocean. The tide, now, had turned, leaving the shore littered with driftwood. Stranded fish and great sea clams cluttered the sand. And there, too, lay lobster buoys, tossed up from far away by the storm. The shore, that should have been smooth with the withdrawal of the water in the ebbing tide, was covered with sea wrack.

The shape of the coast had been changed by the storm. As the day passed and news came to us from all parts of the Cape, we heard tales of a new channel that had appeared in the shore line at Orleans, of the complete disappearance of land on Nantucket Sound, and of deep erosion of the dunes further down the Cape.

One night had altered the map of Cape Cod. The ocean had taken its toll. Enticed by the storm, ravenously it had devoured the land, as it had been doing way back over the centuries, seizing one part and at the same time silting up another, till the Cape became unpredictable of contour.

16

As I returned inland I began to notice further ravages. They were lesser ones, and of little concern to the Cape as a whole. The needles of the pines had started to turn brown from the salt spray tossed far by the wind. But above all this I was conscious of a queer, sickly sweet scent upon the air. I had been vaguely aware of it since first I came into the open. It was a scent that reminded me of sweet hay, or tea. I wondered about it, and then, as I noticed the slashed branches covering the ground, I realized that the perfume came from mutilated leaves of the honey locust. The air was thick with the scent, nostalgic and overly sweet.

We had survived the storm. The outsiders were beginning to feel a bit ashamed of their panic, for nobody had been killed and little damage had been done. Some great trees had fallen before the force of the blow, and the town trucks were busily clearing the roads of broken limbs and tree trunks. Gardens were smashed, and big branches sprawled across the countryside.

But the fishermen were, as usual, philosophically calm and patient. What, after all, was a small squall like this? Their boats were safe. They were alive. To men who had been reared in the tradition and knowledge of storms at sea, all this was of little importance. Disaster, to them, meant shipwrecks. It meant drowned fishermen—ten, twenty, thirty and even forty at a time—with the town in mourning for its sons and husbands, and crepe hanging on every door. That was the only thing that mattered. The land itself would never betray them. It would change its shape, and a dune might be devoured before their eyes; but it would always be there.

The fishermen were busy that morning, bringing their boats back from the safety of Duck Creek, up behind Shirttail Point.

As I remembered this experience, I began to think of another storm here on Cape Cod. It was the storm that broke one of the most intense heat waves I have ever known. That afternoon the heat had mounted in force, till we felt that it was almost more than we could bear. We dared not go to the beach, even, to swim, for the sand was too hot to cross. It was a frightening, solid heat.

I was spending the evening with friends in Truro. During that evening I watched a change come into the sky, where a dull, sullen ochre covered the sunset. This tension could not possibly continue much longer. Something, somewhere, would have to break.

"It's coming," I told them. "I can feel it, all through me. And it's going to be the kind of a storm that one sees just once in a lifetime."

Cape Cod storms—tempests, as the people call them when they include thunder and lightning—hold a special quality of drama. Here, where the land is flat and low, it is like being at sea. The heavens are open to view. We can see them in their majesty, the horizon a complete circle around us.

Suddenly the entire sky turned from ochre to the color of lead. The white houses on the moors stood out weirdly stark against it. And then, as in obedience to a celestial command, all the grasses bent low, one way, in a violent wind. It was the ordered movement in a dance, so unresisting and supple and drilled was everything that grew upon this earth.

It was not long until the lightning began. I had never supposed there could be so many colors in lightning: pink, mauve, steelblue, pale yellow, white; fiercely and in wild abandon it tossed its spears across the heavens.

"You'd better stay here," suggested my friends.

But I knew better. This drive home was going to be something I would always remember. Fear, tonight, was forgotten. I wanted to watch the skies open before me and around me, in these fantastic flings of lightning.

18

I have never seen such a tempest. It was as though the heavens were torn apart in jagged rage.

Then the rain came. It came down in solid sheets.

That night I watched the earth change from tortured, arid heat to gentled, wet coolness, filled with a sense of peaceful release. And with the light of morning the birds sang once more, after weeks of silence.

Ponds

"One of these days, when we both have the time, I'll take you up a high hill where we can see seven ponds."

Many years ago an old fisherman made this promise to me. Like all Cape Codders, he loved the ponds and knew by instinct the people who would understand and share this love.

The years passed. Every time we met we reminded each other of our plan.

"But when?" we would ask. "When shall we go?"

Something always seemed to prevent us. As old Joseph talked of this view over the seven ponds—slowly reeling off their names, with obvious delight in each one of them: Gull, Williams, Higgins, Slough, Horseleech, Herring and one of the many Round Ponds to be found here on the Cape—always, I noticed, a sense of awe came into his voice. It began to look as though he almost feared the realization of the promise.

For a summer would not truly have been a summer if we had not been able to linger, with a sentimental nod of the head in the general direction of those ponds, as we said: "One of these days we'll go there. Yes, one of these days."

If we could not enjoy this thought I believe we would have felt lonely, as though the bond between us had been severed.

But we played too long with time.

This past summer old Joseph died. And now, though I know perfectly well the exact hill he meant, I shall not go there. That hilltop belonged to him, with its view of the chain of ponds. I must respect the glow that came into his face as he talked of it—talked of it as though it were something almost Biblical, something with which to tempt me, something beyond description.

I can see it in my mind, though. The ground would be thick with bearberry, shining silver in the sun, turning dull crimson in the fall, with the scarlet berries glowing among the tiny leaves. Below, and even around us on the hilltop itself, so that we would have had to sweep aside a few of the branches to look at the view of the ponds, down there the stunted pines would cover the land, smelling richly resinous on a summer's day. Perhaps, too, in the white sand at our feet there would be the yellow-flowering cactus, with its prickly fruit. And the silence would have been broken by the regular thump of the breakers at the far side of the hill.

All this I know, though I have never been there.

Actually, I believe I have seen them from a plane. Soon after leaving Provincetown I passed over a straggling chain of ponds, close to the ocean. They were fantastically blue and incredibly transparent beneath me. I saw these ponds as Joseph in his days upon this earth had never been able to see them.

But that was not at all the same thing. Nothing seen from the air holds the intimate magic of a gradual approach from the land, walking to it upon one's own feet over the rim of a hill. And so, with complete integrity, I can say I have respected my tryst with the old fisherman.

Thinking of his love for the ponds, I have wondered why, in this land which is surrounded by water, we should feel as we do about our ponds. It is the recollection of the gentleness on Joseph's face when he talked about them that has given me a possible explanation.

They are our comfort and our security. Over on the back shore, where the Atlantic stretches to Spain, there can never be a sense of tranquility. And even in the bay of Cape Cod the world of water can be ruthless and fraught with danger.

If you are a Cape Codder you need water, for you have always lived against it. And so what happens? There, inland, safely bounded by wooded banks, lie the ponds. They are secret and hidden. They do not stretch into the unknown, the untraveled, the feared. They go round and round and round. You can forget, for a little while, the terror of waves and storms.

So secret are the ponds, whether they be large or small, that there is a feeling of indecency when they become exposed. Recently, when the new main highway was built down the spine of the Cape, unexpected ponds appeared by the side of this highway. The surrounding undergrowth, like a protecting ruffle around their shores, had been stripped from them by the ruthless bulldozers. They were ponds that had been hidden over the centuries, accessible only with the greatest difficulty. There were no paths that led to these ponds, and not many people, outside of the real

23

Cape Codders, had known of their existence, for few would take the trouble to discover them across wild, uncultivated country, with bullbriar tall above the knee and ooze deep beneath the feet. High bush blueberries had edged these ponds, and the wild white azalea and the flowering sweet pepper had scented the air in late July. The banks were steep, the bed of the black water correspondingly deep. Sometimes, in these especially steep-banked ponds, you had the feeling that there must be truth in the old legends which held that certain of the ponds were actually bottomless. Frightening legends they were, telling of people who had fallen into these ponds and whose bodies have never again been seen.

But perhaps there is another reason for our delight in ponds. This is the only water on the Cape that is independent of the discipline of the tides. We can swim here without having to remember whether it is high or low tide. For a little while, we can surrender ourselves to unchanging serenity.

It is a gentle, intimate world. I lived for a few weeks overlooking one of these ponds. Less than a hundred feet from the ocean, its water was completely fresh. No salt from the sea ever seeped up into it. Regularly each evening, as the surface of the pond yellowed under the sunset sky, I saw this smooth surface rippled by a stag, his doe and their fawn. So punctual was the little family, as it tripped down the hill and across the bottom land to its drinking pool, that I began to use its arrival as the signal for starting to cook my supper. The stag would lift his head high, to sniff the air. But I was sheltered from them by the closed windows of the house. During the day, as I walked around the pond, I noticed that the creatures had worn a path to their drinking place; the marshy ooze at the edge of the water was cut up by their feet till it looked as though someone had come along with a hoe, to cultivate this land for planting. Over those weeks of my stay I began to love that

24

pond, growing very possessive about it. And I found myself understanding why so many of our ponds carry the names of the families who have lived upon their shores; it does not take long for one to identify oneself with a particular pond. There is a sense of secrecy and privacy which merges into a feeling of ownership.

It must seem good to have a pond named after you—a pond or a hollow: Cahoon or Newcomb, Dyer, Bassett, Sears, Higgins, Snow or Williams. This is surely the best and most benign form of immortality: to leave your mark upon the map of a land. The history of Cape Cod lies hidden behind these names.

But the ponds are also named for their particular shapes, or for something characteristic about them. And so, here on the outer Cape, we have Long Pond and Great Pond, Round Pond and Gull Pond—Gull Pond with the perpetual white chaplet of gulls resting upon the center of its water, seeming never to move or fly away. But why, I have often wondered, is there a Slough Pond? Is this some toss back to the world of *Pilgrim's Progress*, with its Slough of Despond? Duck Pond one can understand, and Turtle Pond, too, for ducks and turtles are everywhere to be seen. And Spectacle Pond exactly resembles a pair of glasses. But does Horseleech Pond really mean what its name suggests? I have always feared so, and only with the greatest hesitation have I dared even to wade there. I would never dream of swimming there, having actually heard that leeches, or blood suckers, live in it.

There are many stories of how these ponds have changed their nature over the years. The waywardness of water takes control, playing tricks with the shape of our land. Aided by the fall of leaves from the trees, it clogs the passageway between the ponds; bottoms come up and the level of the ponds, which are no longer able to flow so freely outward into these passageways, rises. Many of the ponds are landlocked and have no outlet. But the particular chain I know best—Gull, Higgins, Williams and Herring—still keeps open its link with the sea.

And thus it is that we can watch the spawning of the herring. Up the winding little Herring River come the alewives, punctually in the month of May, obeying a race instinct that can surmount all obstacles. Swimming against the current—for the Herring River flows out into the bay of Cape Cod, from this chain of ponds—the herring enter into the region of the land down at the Gut, near Wellfleet. Through the flapper valve there they pass, up into the Herring River itself, which flows among the low-lying meadows and swamps, soon to be transformed into a pink carpet of wild roses, and, later in the year, to bear all the berries that anyone could desire. Under the fantastic little High Toss Bridge they swim, and around Merrick Island, till they go over the sluice and reach the seclusion of Gull Pond. It is a typically heroic saga of reproduction, this spawning of the herring, filled with life instinct and the awareness of self-preservation.

And there around the shores of Gull Pond we can see them, in May, June and even into very early July. If you watch the pond you will notice that the smooth surface is agitated into strange round balls of water. This means that the spawning is taking place, in groups of eight or ten circles of disturbed water.

They are running into the ponds in their multitudes, just now, in early summer, and the shores are dedicated to this dance of breeding. Seven or eight or even a dozen females group together for the laying of the eggs, while the males swish around them in these grouped circles, fertilizing the eggs with the milt. The stillness of Gull Pond is wrinkled by this seminal agitation.

Throughout the summer the life instinct continues. Early September comes, and the three-inch-long young alewives, with the parent fish, begin to get the seasonal urge to move on somewhere,

26

away from the security of the pond. And it is now that an extra sense of cautious awareness seems to enter into them. Was the summer hot and dry? This means that the passageway between the ponds, on the way down the Herring River to the open bay, disturbingly shallow at best, is perilously low and unduly warm. Better wait, instinctively reason the multitudes of herring. Better wait until the next rainfall, when the streams are higher and cooler. And so they wait, these thousands upon thousands of alewives, in a season of drought, intuitively aware of danger.

The rains come. They may not come until late in the fall or early in winter. But the fish know their moment. They know when they will no longer have difficulty in passing through these shallow streams. And they go, anywhere from early September to February, leaving the ponds waiting and ready for the next generation the following summer.

But behind them they leave their sister fish, the fresh-water trout, who have driven out the bass, the pickerel and the perch. These trout live upon the young alewives, waiting and watching as the little ones leap high into the air, as though on tiptoe, to catch the tiny white flies.

All this is the world of the fisherman.

But the world of birds around these ponds holds its own richness. Live here sometime and you will discover them. There are vicious, dramatic birds; the woods are filled with the great horned owls, a full two feet high, these night feeders who delight in living upon the skunk. And should you want to watch the interplay of nature, you can delight in the way the crows gang up on these great horned owls, as they sit upon their perches in the stunted pines. They pick upon them as they flock around them, heckling, till the owls, in desperation, are chased from their perches to a far away place of resting. There are American Eagles, too, I have been told—though never have I been fortunate enough to see them—nesting in the wildness of Featherbed Swamp, near Truro. And the magic moment arrives, in the middle of October, when thick skeins of Canada geese pass over the Cape on their passage south. They stop off, to rest and feed at night, upon the shore line of Gull Pond.

Civilization, however it may try, is having a hard time to subdue this world of the ponds here on Cape Cod.

But, unless you chance to be a fervent fisherman, one of the greatest delights of living near these ponds lies in swimming. I have watched the joy of a swimmer in early morning, tossing pure silver into the air around him from the cut water: an alchemist, he appeared, able to make silver from water, shaping it with each turn of his arm in the crawl, as he crossed the pond, catching the light of the rising sun. And I have swum across the same pond at sunset, in molten gold. The water, against the rich, deep pink gold, by contrast seemed strangely cold. And then, as I dived beneath this molten surface, I found a world that was a cool, pale green.

Swimming in these ponds holds the strangest and most unexpected surprises. One day, I remember, I dived, in the excitement of wearing my new goggles, which revealed to me an entire world of which I had, hitherto, known nothing. I dived deep, among the weird forests of growth that are rooted in the bed of the ponds —furry-edged, upward-pointing plants that are so much more exciting beneath the surface of the water than they are when they appear above, as mere flat leaves or insignificant vegetation. Below this water I saw plant growth of a richness I had never imagined. But, too, I saw other things of yet greater magic. Diving down to the bed of this pond, among the little turtles that rested upon submerged tree stumps, surrounded by the tiny, almost transparent fish that darted around me as I swam, there, suddenly, I found the bones and the antlers of a stag. And with this discovery I felt the sudden poignancy of conjecture. When had this tragedy happened? I imagined the desperate spring of the creature into the pond. Was he being chased during the one short week of the annual hunting season? But why did he not swim to shore? And how far back in time did this take place? I tried to extricate the antlers from the tangle of tree stump and weed, hoping to bring them ashore as trophies. But then I thought better of it. Leave them there, I decided. Leave them where rightly they belonged, safe beneath the water of this pond.

Up against these bony remains of the stag lay the broken branch of some great tree. It was old cedar, of a mighty size that must have belonged to the era, many hundreds of years ago, when the Cape was a thick forest with noble stands of trees—trees that were shaped into the sailing ships of New England, trees our ancestors failed to respect and willfully destroyed, so that the Cape, today, is barren of forest.

But, too, there are gentler, equally sweet delights. I swim in a pond, among the water lilies, picking them as I pass, my feet entangled in the long, lank stems, my hands confused with lily pads. Or I watch these ponds in the moonlight, and the silver path of the moon moves slowly and with deliberation across the surface of the water. Better still, I swim in this moonlight.

Fog appears. It rises suddenly, sometimes, even as we are out in the center of a pond in a row boat. And there is an air of frightening mystery in this formless world. It is almost as terrifying as being caught in a fog upon the flats. But here, one knows, land is near. Always one can manage to reach it.

Thick white fog rises from the ponds at the approach of the fall. It rises in the precise forms of the ponds themselves, so that, even though the moon may be shining, yet one is lost. Look down upon these hollows, filled with the water of the ponds, and you will see shapes of white—round, or long, or irregular, according to which particular pond they cloak.

Tideless and serene, the ponds yet change with the seasons, reflecting the mood of the sky above them or the quality of the air itself. Ultramarine in high summer, slate-gray under a stormy sky, with white tops even in a strong wind, orange at sunset, mist-veiled in fog and cold: they vary with the swing of the year. And, as we live by them, aware of the sense of security they give to us, we know we are living against something that goes back to the very beginning of our land when the glacial ice melted and sank deep into the kettle holes of Cape Cod, and gave us our ponds.

The Blessing of the Fleet

The town has been in a state of flutter for some time. Along the edge of the shore, in every boat yard and dock, the draggers and line trawlers are being cleaned and painted. *Sea Fox, Queen Mary, Judy* and *Tony, Johnny Boy, Cap'n Bill* and *Papa Joe:* scores of little newly painted fishing boats gleam and sparkle in the late June sun.

Inside the gray, shingled houses of the Portuguese fishermen the women work, getting ready the flags and pennants for the boats: stripes of white, blue, orange, green and red; checked flags; pennants bright with triangles and bands of shouting color.

When you walk along the streets of Provincetown you can

feel a seething excitement. It has a strange quality, as though it is something that has been going on in the unconscious for a long time, only now to come to the surface. It is the consummation of an unstated need.

The fishermen of Provincetown prepare for the first ceremony of the Blessing of the Fleet.

Everything must have a beginning. Each myth and legend, all folk songs and ballads, started at some moment in time. In Europe the pattern of mythology is ancient and deeply ingrained. There the people take for granted the saints and miracles, the festivals and songs. But here in the New World, where we are still young, we have the excitement of shaping our legends and myths.

Today, on this last Sunday in June—the time of year of so many religious fiestas in the Old World, when, on the eve of St. John, the priest blesses the fishermen and the olive fields in the Mediterranean, that cradle of these very Portuguese fishermen of Provincetown who hold below awareness the race memory of their ancestors—on this last Sunday in June, the fishermen are initiating a ceremony that will link the Old World with the New.

The day contains within the cup of its hours the essential elements of magic. It is a merging of the sacred into the Bacchic, filled with color and noise, holy silence and final abandon. It belongs both to ancient and modern: the era of the primitive and the mechanisation of our own century.

And, as it should, the ceremony begins with the fishermen's Mass.

A procession forms before the town hall, marching through the narrow streets, winding its way up and down little connecting lanes till finally it reaches the church. It is a loud, trumpeting procession, gaudy in color as it is brassy in sound. It is mankind praising his Maker in noises, as immemorially he has done. Watching it, you feel that God, undeniably sitting up there in the blue summer sky, cannot help but love with a smiling compassion these mortals who glorify him in this rowdy manner.

But despite the noise, it is an orderly, organized procession, headed by three standard bearers, their dual allegiance symbolized by the carrying of two Stars and Stripes' and one Portuguese flag.

And then comes the band of the American Legion. Uniformed in deep blue and black and gold, the players wear high tufted plumes on their headdresses. Upon the trumpets and the trombones and the tubas they play the Thunderer March with such sweating exuberance of blown-out cheeks that the whole of Provincetown must vibrate with the music. The band is led by a drum majorette in a white satin dress, high above her knees, disclosing gorgeously sexy young thighs. With her bare legs and arms and the tossing plumes on her head, she twirls her baton and twists and shakes her hips, till she seems to embody the desires of man.

She is a beautiful girl, and somehow in a strange way there is nothing discordant about her. For everything this morning is praising its Creator: spirit, soul and body. And what does it matter that suddenly one is flung into the mood of a college football game? For there, standing at the entrance to the church of the holy Saint Peter, patron of fishermen, where the Mass is to be celebrated, there, standing with such dignity, sanctified and filled with wisdom, is the sedate old Bishop in his crimson robes, encircled by priests and little choirboys.

Into the church files the procession: the Fourth Degree Knights of Columbus, looking like sleek, well-fed red-wing blackbirds with their shiny, crimson-lined black cloaks, and carrying in their white-gloved hands the silver swords. But behind them come the Portuguese fishermen, the real reason for this ceremony. High in

33

the air before them they bear the purple, gold-fringed banners, embroidered with the names of their boats. Foiled by the black cloaks of the Knights of Columbus, their check work-shirts glow like a garden of marigolds and zinnias.

And they carry these colors into the little church, where the summer sun streams through the windows and the open doors with such force that it dims the lights of the candles within. Sitting there, closely clumped in the pews and catching the light of the sun, the fishermen resemble a great stained-glass window spread across the body of the church, the colors of the check shirts—orange and green, blue, crimson and yellow—running up into the colors of the robes of the saints in the windows, and being repeated in the deep crimson and blue of the votive lights.

They sit there quietly during the Mass, these fiercely dark-skinned men of action, these sun-tanned Portuguese fishermen with deep furrows in the skin of their brown necks, which have been weathered by storms at sea. The dark brown pales the silver chains holding the holy medals around their necks and contrasts with the pink tops of balding heads, which have been shielded from the sun by their caps. As they lean their tattooed, brown arms across the backs of the pews, you are aware of the collective muscled strength of these men with bodies toughened by labor. And turning your eyes from them suddenly towards the altar, you receive the full impact of the sugary-white angels, standing there so cold in their carved marble.

At the end of a pew on the further aisle sits the drum majorette, her bare limbs golden against the white satin of her dress. But the fishermen pay no heed to her. They are listening to the "Ave Maria" sung high up in the gallery by a soprano, as though it came from Heaven itself; and as they listen, these simple Latins in a Northern land, the emotionalism of their race wells up till strong,

34

hardened men can be seen to rub the tears from their eyes.

And now the priest is talking to them. He is telling them about the beauty and dignity of their work. He reminds them of The Divine Fisherman, Who loved and understood the sea and the men of ships.

"You who have abandoned your boats and left your nets at the busiest season to come unto God today. . . ."

The fishermen seem to swell with humble pride in their calling. Throughout the church one feels a wave of elation so strong that it is almost visible. And as the pale-faced priest goes on talking to them of the joys and riches and sorrows of the deep, it is almost as though one were carried out beyond this building and tossed upon the Atlantic in a Northeaster, fishing off Georges Bank. Here, to-day, the fishermen know that they matter; and when one of their company offers himself as a symbol of the fleet, and receives the communion, you are sure that this entire body of men feels sanctified and fed. They know they will ride the seas in greater safety through the power of this Mass.

It is early afternoon of the same day. The festival has become general and the crowds have gathered on the town wharf for the actual ceremony of the Blessing of the Fleet—crowds in their many thousands, as the newspapers later said, crowds from off-Cape, summer visitors, city folk, as well as the families of the fishermen and the true Cape Codders. The sun has gone behind the clouds and, in the dull light that becomes Provincetown so well —for it is a silvery town, subtle in its grays, and looks its best when the weather mood is subdued—in this cloudy light colors seem doubly rich. You can scarcely see the fishing boats, they are so covered with pennants and flags. A southwest breeze stiffens, and uncountable flags and pennants flutter. Everything seems to sway with a rhythmic movement: boats on the water, flags on the boats; even the crowds on the wharf, as they wander over the scene, and the men selling the colored balloons, looking like bunches of brilliant, wind-tossed flowers.

But let us go closer to the draggers concealed behind the fugue of flags. Along there is the Virgin's boat. She carries a sail painted with a picture of Our Lady descending in pink clouds: two women kneel beneath her, and a man dressed in a shirt and pants, tending a gawky sheep, raises his hands in adoration. Her boat is brilliant cerulean blue; her dories are colored orange. Further along the wharf is another dragger, dedicated to Saint Peter. This boat, too, has a painted sail; on it is a figure of Saint Peter, in blue and red, and around the figure are wreathed the words "Hail St. Peter, Patron of Fishermen."

And now the crowd has parted, to make way for the procession. Once again the standard bearers, the American Legion Band, and the Knights of Columbus introduce the bright-shirted fishermen. And once again the air is filled with the sound of trumpets and trombones. But now, this afternoon, the noise is far greater and more abandoned. For, into the brassy music of the band itself is added the tooting of whistles from all the fishing boats, as well as the hooting of hundreds of cars, sirens from everywhere and even the roar of airplanes in the sky. It is a world of benign confusion and movement: movement of color in the wind-fluttered flags, in the milling crowds, in the gay procession; movement of sounds, vivid and various.

But this afternoon the procession does not end with the fishermen. They are followed by priests and altar boys, arrayed in gold and scarlet and lace that compete in vain with the gaudy colors of the check work-shirts.

Standing here on the town wharf, I notice an old woman beside me, dressed in black. As I glance towards her she smiles at me and seems to want to talk. There is a sad wisdom in her face, lifting her above the gaiety of the scene before us. And as we talk, I learn that she is the widow of a fisherman and the mother of fishermen. The festival is bringing back memories.

"It's a hard life," she murmurs to me, her voice scarcely audible above the toots and whistles and sirens. "It's a hard life, I tell you. They come back home so tired, so worn out and wet, with blood-shot eyes. I remember when my first little girl was just going to be born."

Saying this, she turns to a richly buxom young woman by her side, full-blown like a flower, with the dark beauty of the Portuguese.

"Yes," goes on the fisherman's widow. "It was the time when she was just going to be born. He'd been at sea for three weeks and had had no catch. It was tough, I tell you. It was tough, cheering him up just when I myself was needing it."

Thinking of this woman beside me, I feel a rush of great tenderness towards these fishermen. And with this tenderness I seem to understand the meaning of what I am watching.

But at this moment I am aware of a sudden hush. The Bishop is arriving.

It seems strange, seeing him in an automobile. By now I am so completely absorbed into this festival that I almost expect him to descend from the sky in flames of fire. He should, at the very least, be borne high into our midst on a rich litter. At first impact this car seems a discordant anachronism. And then I see the falseness of my reaction.

I realize that today's ceremonies must belong to our own age. It is our responsibility to create the setting for contemporary festivals and legends. We must be able to instill a sense of magic into the automobile and the airplane. We need to create gods of the silo and contour plowing, of the outboard-motor boat and the vehicles of twentieth-century speed. Ritualism and magic are not mere remnants of a past age. They belong here and now, to everything around us.

Feeling this, I find myself rejoicing in the arrival of the Bishop in his car.

Now there is a complete silence. Coming after the noise it seems almost to be a loud silence, it is so intense.

The silence continues as the Bishop in his robes mounts the platform and blesses the entire fishing fleet.

And then the fishermen board their boats. They cast off to make the circle of the harbor, and the air is filled once again with noise. This time it is loud with the chug of engines being started up as the boats fan out in an arc that takes them almost as far as Long Point, and brings them around then, slowly, one by one, to the town wharf, for the Bishop's individual blessing.

Night falls, blotting out the colors of the flags. But darkness brings a new enchantment, as lights appear in the little boats. Masts vanish upwards into the stars, and black hulks are doubled black, into black water. But this inky blackness is broken and confused with lights—lights that wriggle and twirl in the gentle sway of the boats till they look like serpents of gold upon the dark sea. And these same lights play havoc with the life upon the little fishing craft, distorting and obscuring everything and everyone, till it is a demon world which we inhabit. The Virgin no longer descends in rose-colored clouds upon her painted sail; significantly she is hidden in thick shadow, shadow tossed upon her by the table of food and drinks that has been set up on the deck of her special trawler.

For the Bacchanalia has begun. True to race memory and faithful to tradition, the day ends in a flurry of feasting. The fishermen entertain upon their boats. They celebrate in the manner of workers upon the land or the sea, the world over. And they eat, drink and dance with the particular security of release that comes to them from the feeling of having been specially hallowed and blessed.

Far into the night the fishermen and their friends eat and drink thus, yet the opened hatches seem still to disclose unending supplies of clams, shrimp and lobster, watermelon, beer and special Portuguese sweet bread. The world is benign and conquerable; there is nothing to fear. And in this mood of fearlessness, the constriction of one boat frets them, till suddenly they need to celebrate with all the boats anchored here against the town wharf. As though at a given, invisible, inaudible signal, some of the younger figures are seen to dive into that black water, wriggling with golden snakes, to clamber into neighbor boats and make links in this chain of celebration.

Night passes and pales into dawn. A tiredness spreads. It is a good tiredness, and a rightful tiredness. Man's day has been complete. He has worshipped and been blessed. He has rejoiced and he has belonged with the fellowship of his brother fishermen. Dancing, eating and drinking, filled with rowdy merriment and sanctified joy, he is exhaustedly assured that life is good. And, in his dim awareness, worn out from the long hours of the day's festivities, he knows that he has appeased all his gods. He is ready to face the cruel sea off Georges Banks. No longer, at this moment, does he fear the force of the northeaster. And his women, sitting proudly upon his boat, know that they hold the courage that is asked of all the women of fishermen everywhere, since the beginning of recorded time.

It has been a good day, and a day charged with magic.

The Magic of the Flats

The best time to learn the world of the flats comes at the full of the moon. Then, for a few days in the Bay of Cape Cod, the big tides run high—nearly twelve feet at their peak—and, with the correspondingly extreme low, the water retreats far into the bay, exposing land that is never seen over the rest of the month.

This dramatically low tide occurs early in the day, when the morning light is clean and clear, giving a pearly beauty to the world.

The mud flats are forsaken and desolate, frequented only by a scattering of quahog rakers. During the summer, when the Cape is filled with vacationists, you seldom find any of the visitors out there. To them the sea is something in which to swim. When it withdraws from them at low tide, they wait until the water returns. And this is fortunate, for some of the special quality of the flats lies in the eerie solitude.

The flats hold a subtle, rather than an obvious, beauty. It is the beauty of uncountable gradations of tone and hue, of the sheen and polish of exposed wet sand at low water. It is a world of reflections upon the wet sand from the slanted light of the morning sky.

There is a sense of vastness on such a morning. This stretch of mud and sand, merging imperceptibly in the far distance into remote water, seems to extend into eternity. In such a light, time and space become intermingled; we can no longer distinguish one from the other.

But it is not only the muted, opalescent coloring of the wet sand, shimmering and glinting upon the bed of the withdrawn ocean, that holds such magic. There are uncountable variations of form here, too. For this is the whole earth in microcosm, with Lilliputian valleys and hills, gorges and plateaux. It might be said to be a child's world, everything within the grasp of the hand, the range of the eye. To the right, past Otto the Finn's stranded dory, sucked deep into the sand and half-filled with water, the rope of its anchor lying curved and loose, over there the ocean bed must be definitely deeper, for always, I notice, however low the tide, a tiny river flows swiftly around the cliffs of the sand. Against the diminutive setting it might be a Ganges or a Mississippi. Wade in this miniature river and the water is cool and clear, in contrast to the warm mud of the flats.

The flats are threaded with these tiny rivulets following the course of the channels they have eroded. They are evident only at the moment of low tide. As I wade in them, though, I am reminded of the sudden, abruptly cool currents in the water of the bay

42

when I swim at high tide; they must surely be caused by these same cold channels. The rivulets flow in narrow streams, twisting around the raised sand. Suddenly they broaden into mighty lakes, full fifteen feet wide.

And then we walk out on these flats, so muddy that the feet sink deep beneath the surface, into soft black ooze. Seen from a distance they appear devoid of all life, and all interest. But what do we discover? This is no dead world of mud. It is a living, agitated world, filled with pulsating rhythm and movement. Scarcely anything here lies motionless, except the long-vacated, sharp-edged shells of oysters and clams, clumped upright in the wet sand and looking as prehistoric as Stonehenge.

Stand still in your path across this mud. The flats appear to move. They heave. They vibrate. And then you hear a strange sound against the silence around. It is a sucking sound, and for a moment I wonder what it is that I am reminded of. Suddenly I am removed from this watery world. I am tossed backwards in time, far inland, upon the chalk downs of southern England in the spring of the year. I am watching with the bearded old shepherd as the newborn lambs nuzzle their dams. Further back in time and I am a child, crouching in the kennels in the back garden as the latest litter of puppies suckles the mother dog. It is a warm sound, and strange that it should come from this cold, watery setting. Suck, suck, suck, goes the sound. Suck, suck, suck.

Puzzled, I raise my eyes to the flats. Thin jets of water spout before me, like tiny fountains. The air sparkles as the sun catches them, tossing into them the colors of the rainbow. Sometimes they are flung far, and this spectrum-tinted water, bewitched by the early morning sun, describes great arcs across the mud.

What is it that causes this crazy happening?

It is the scallops. They lie here, countless in their numbers.

At this moment, when I am confused, still, by sight and sound and strange recollections from the past, the shellfish warden approaches me across the flats.

"A good scallop year," he informs me blandly, not knowing how he has smashed my fantasies. "Never seen so many scallops —not for years I haven't. Looks to me as if we'll have a real bumper season, come October and they've grown."

And then I see what is happening. It is a world of *Alice in Wonderland*, with the Walrus and the Carpenter and the Oysters. The uncountable scallops assume a fairy-tale quality, till you would feel little surprise were they suddenly to develop legs and feet and should walk and talk. They open and shut their shells, like a multitude of castanets, like a gigantic audience applauding the beauty of this earth on such a morning in late June.

But, too, they have a rude aspect to their behavior; they spit, as they open, in the manner of vulgar old men. They yawn, exposing that mighty muscle which is the part that we eat. Along the rim of each beautiful fluted shell they boast a row of brilliant turquoise-blue, green-edged, jewel-like eyes. Give them the slightest kick as they lie here in the mud at low tide, and they will retaliate by spitting you in the face. They imagine they are beneath the water, still, opening and shutting to breathe and propel themselves along the bay.

The scallop is never static. It is far more active and flexible than the heavy, uncouth quahog that noses its way downward into the mud and sand of the water bed. It has an adventurous spirit. The entire bay is its universe. And it is as beautiful of shape as it is mobile of movement, a delicate, graceful creature, the fluted shells subtly varied in color. And with this beauty it carries, too, the sense of history in its background; for did not the pilgrims of the Middle Ages adopt it as their symbol of pilgrimage?

44

Sometimes this sucking sound changes to a wheezing, squeezing noise, as the scallops force out the water before them, the better to propel themselves along. They do not even await disturbance, as does the razor fish, but act independently of all outside happenings.

Nothing is still here upon the flats, except the discarded clam and oyster shells; and even these ancient creatures are peopled with tiny sea snails perching on top of them, like Kings of the Castle in the game of a child. Over the floor of the sea swarm the hermit crabs, so minute and so active, trotting around on nervous little feet, or retiring into their shells to get sucked down deep into the bed of the wet sand. They creep among the colorless slabs of jellyfish, and the stranded shells, dull of hue against the rich scarlet of the frilly edged sponge that encrusts the oysters and clams.

And then, in a sudden little dip of sand, I see two crabs. They face each other caressingly. The larger one is deep dark brown, with yellow markings; he has beautiful sage-green legs. He faces the smaller, softer-toned crab, and, as I look at them, casting aside any scientific explanation, I like to feel they must be lovers, for they lie so close and so happily entwined. Mischievously I touch the big one with my foot, and he stirs and stretches. But then, within a short moment, he beds down once more, easing himself into the soft cushion of the sand, like a dog settling to sleep. I leave them in their embrace, upon a cold wet nuptial couch.

This morning the shallow water of the channels seems filled with crabs. Never have I come across so many. They wander around my feet, giving me occasional vicious little nips; there are big drab-colored fellows, a few prehistoric-looking horseshoe crabs, dwarfing the others by their enormous size, but chiefly the smaller, gayer-colored creatures, cavorting along upon the bed of the water with tremendous speed.

The fishermen are out here in the bay, raking for quahogs. Otto, the elderly Finn, has arrived. He goes to his stranded dory. He bales the water from the boat, one booted leg within the dory and the other one high in the air, behind him, as he leans over with the baler. Next he collects his rake and the wire-net basket to hold the quahogs and then, in the rubber boots high up his thighs— these enormous boots that make him look so disproportionately spindly of figure, like some queer water beetle—he slooshes out to the channel that separates the shore from Egg Island. Soon he is busily raking, turning the quahogs over into the net basket below the water. Doubled in this shallow water, his reflection makes the channel seem far deeper than it really is.

The shellfish warden is watchful, these days of the early morning high course tides. He is on the look out for anyone who may come quahogging without the necessary license.

"It makes me mad," he tells me. "It burns me up, the way the summer people seem to think they can rob us fishermen of our shellfish. It's our livelihood they're taking from us, if they only knew it. And they just seem to think the clams are there for their particular pleasure."

Over the months of summer you can see him, at the moment of low tide, searching the flats with his keen eyes for the pilferers of the quahog and oyster.

"And not only that," he goes on. "They even rake our beds."

He nods his head towards the staked out beds. There, upon the flats, stand the thin, upright saplings, bounding the beds. A few of them, on more recent beds, or supplanting worn-out stakes, carry unwithered oak leaves upon their branches, strangely incongruous against the sand and sea.

And then suddenly and unexpectedly the warden's face breaks into a broad grin. He has lost his severity.

48

"Talking of beds," he says, "did I ever tell you that story—the story of when I was courting? I was a grouchy old bachelor in those days, living alone at the water's edge. And my girl's mother came along once with her to visit me—just to see what sort of a fellow I was, I do believe, living there all by myself. No sooner had they arrived and looked around my shack, but they must leave in a hurry and a rush. Sort of confused, the mother was. And it was only many years later, after we'd been married and all, that I found out what it was about. It was my licenses—my bed licenses pinned there, all around the walls. 'Bed licenses,' says my future mother-in-law to her daughter. 'And what sort of a man do you think you're about to marry, so brazen that he has bed licenses stuck there, all around him. Regular fast character, he must be, I tell you. Not the sort of man I'd like my daughter to marry.' But then, she was a city woman, she was. Couldn't really expect her to know anything about shellfish, could you? But it might have broken my marriage, though."

He is in a communicative mood. There are no intruders this morning, and he has little to do.

"And the way these summer people think they have to take a rake for the quahogs," he says with a slight sneer. "If they could only see the holes the quahogs make, like tiny worm holes in the flats, they could just pick them up. That's what we fishermen do. But these summer people, they just can't seem to see the holes. Their eyesight isn't good enough."

I find myself wanting to remind him that old Otto—surely one of the most venerable of fishermen—uses a rake. But I decide to keep silent.

He kicks some oyster shells at his feet.

"Not that I'm much concerned over quahogs," he goes on. "It's really the oyster that interests me. That's what Wellfleet used to mean to us all, in the olden days. And we're trying now to bring them back. So long as we can keep the whelk from sucking them we ought to be able to do it. You see that notice, saying the Island's closed? We've been seeding them over there and they're coming back, they are. . . . Like to see something?"

He dives into his pocket and brings out a tiny vitamin-pill glass bottle. Opening it, he shakes out a large shabby pearl.

"See this? I found this pearl in an oyster, one day many years ago. Always take it around with me, just to look at in odd moments, or to show to people like you, who might be interested. A beauty, isn't it? It takes me back to the days when I was young. Used to be able to open twenty gallons of oysters in six hours, at twenty cents a gallon. It's just a knack; that's all it is. Just a knack."

Across the flats, towards the shore line, two figures have appeared. The shellfish warden's eyes are fixed upon them in a sudden rush of suspicion.

"Got to be going now," he says abruptly. "Got to go and see who those people are."

As he leaves me I walk further out into the bay, to join a friend who is raking for quahogs.

We scratch the surface of the mud at the water's edge, or even down into the water-covered channels, for the hard-shelled clam, the quahog, as it is called on the Cape from the days when the Indians lived here and prized it as their food. It is an exciting harvest, like all harvests of the unseen. It is charged with speculation, like the digging of potatoes. Something hard resists the rake and you haul it up, secure between the prongs: there is your quahog. Or you dip your hand down into the muddied water—this water that blackens as you disturb it with the rake or with your feet— and bring it up. The wire basket, sitting there on the bed of the channel, three quarters submerged below the water, grows heavy with the quahogs. We lift it and place it near to our center of opera-tion, as we move across the flats.

When the basket is full to its brim, we carry it to our staked bed. Scratching a shallow hole in the mud, we stick the quahogs verti-cally down, scarcely below the surface. The bed has the appear-ance of a vegetable garden, out here at sea, with its orderly rows. They might almost be onions that we plant, or daffodil bulbs. And now, as we place the clams into their new home, we watch them. After the first moment of stunned resistance they start to react according to their nature. With a gentle rocking movement they get themselves sucked down below the surface of the mud, draw-ing in their siphons and shutting their shells as they force out the water inside them in tiny jets. Come back here in a few more min-utes and you will see nothing. They will have vanished below, set-tling themselves flat within their muddy beds. And all that can be seen will be the oyster shells, planted in this bed, shabby-colored and ancient-looking, so hoary of texture that they seem to antedate time.

The world of the flats has a seasonal element, every bit as much as though it were the vegetable world of dry land, with the bloom-ing and ripening of fruit or grain. The "set" of the oyster takes place in the spring or the early summer, and the little scallops in the bay reach maturity only in October. June and July pass, and I wander over the flats at the end of August. The morning is foggy. I seem to move in space, like a figure in an early Chinese landscape. I have lost all sense of dimension or element. It is already daylight, but the fog makes me recollect a walk I took many years before, at dusk, when the fog rolled in with the suddenness of the dropping of the curtain at the end of a play. That evening, as I stood there upon the flats, well out into the bay, I felt myself to be living upon an uninhabited planet. It was as I would imagine it to be, were I to wander upon the surface of the moon. My feet sank deep into mud, plunging to the calves of my legs. My mind knew that this was black mud, though my eyes could see little of the color. I waded into channels of water, to the knees, water filled with unperceived crabs. And suddenly, as I stood there, knee-deep in water and mud, I felt panic. It was an unashamed, animal panic, the terror of complete loss of direction, an aloneness in space, with the tide turning and the sea advancing, and my not knowing exactly where to walk. In this eerie, scarifying world, formless and lightless, extending into fog, blurred by fog and darkening dusk, I stood still. I searched the sky, but above me was nothing but fog.

"Stupid," I found myself saying. "Nobody in their senses would have done such an idiotic thing. Why, perhaps I'll have to stay here till the incoming tide, with the water lapping higher and higher up my legs and thighs. That will show me where I am. Then I can walk away from it. . . . But suppose I go in circles, as people are supposed to do when they are lost?"

In a queer way I found something exciting in the sense of utter loneliness. I knew that if I were to manage to reach land, I would have experienced something that was worth this panic and fear.

But things always seem to turn out right in the end. At the moment when panic was beginning to envelop me, I stood completely still and very slowly turned myself around. There must have been a sudden break in the thickening fog, for I saw a light in the distance before me. I walked towards it, my eyes fixed upon it, regardless of whether I trod upon crab or sharp-edged oyster shell, or sank deep to my knees in mud. I shall never know how long it took me to reach shore, for I had forsaken the habitual world of dry land, with its sense of time. But I fastened my eyes to that solitary light, till finally I found my feet were treading safely on sand.

All this has come back to me, as I wander across the flats on a foggy morning in late August. But it is a thin fog today, simplifying the curves of Egg Island, dark gray against the silver water. At any moment it will lift, disclosing the form of the flats and the patterning of the cool, swift-running channels. I cross Egg Island, to the far edge, past the green-tinged part that is covered with tattered sea lettuce, and the desolate, lifeless mud gives way to the strangest accumulation of razor fish shells. My feet crunch upon them, in their thousands, mud-obscured, lying there at all angles. And I wonder why it should be that they are here at this particular spot, and nowhere else.

Then, as I look across at this flatness of mud, still infused with a sense of mystery in the silver and opal light, I see larger objects, humped upon the flatness. I go nearer to them to find out what they are. They are something I have never seen before. Each of the humped shapes, looking so large against the absolute flatness around, is a conch, or big winkle or whelk. In themselves they are nothing new; often have I collected the discarded shells along the shore, and know and love the rich whorled shapes and the delicate coloring. But these, here today, are no discarded conchs. They are alive and functioning at this moment in the laying of their eggs.

It is a beautiful, very moving sight, the conch as it spins its necklace of egg discs, fully fifteen inches in length. In some inexplicable fashion it holds a timeless, ageless quality of tender maternity. Against the cold, dead color of mud it glows with a warm pink; the egg discs are flesh color as they emerge from the obtruded mantle of the conch, and before they turn to pale biscuit by exposure to the air they are like the deep pink cream of a baby's skin.

The dignified, majestic mounds of conch shell litter the flats. I tug at one of the egg necklaces, but it is rooted deep into the mud like an umbilical cord. The chain of egg discs is secured along one side as with a strong spun tape, like the binding edge of a ruffle. The necklace twists and curls, from its anchorage in the mud, to the great ugly mass of fleshy folds of the mantle obtruding from the pearly lilac and pinks of the beautiful shell. Upon the back of the ugly flesh, and ready to clamp down when the soft mantle has fulfilled its purpose and shrinks back into its shell, the conch carries the hard, flat lid of its operculum.

The scene before me, here in the cold dark mud, holds all the ambivalent ugliness and beauty of procreation. Out from those clammy-looking folds of flesh emerge the beautiful, lengthy chains of egg discs. Over to the right, beyond the scarlet sponges, I see some necklaces that have been expelled by the conch. Thev will float here, on the incoming tide, secured into the mud, untu the eggs have matured.

Transported by the beauty of what I have seen, I return home from the flats. At my feet I see a tiny baby sturgeon, a mere six inches long, its pointed snout already well defined. But my mind is too full just now. I can scarcely notice the beauty of the gulls, circling the mud, shrieking and mewing in their flight. Before my feet, as I walk across the sand by the fringe of the eel grass, regiments of minute fiddler crabs hurry into the grasses, crackling as they go. The muddy sand is punctured with the holes into which they disappear. And there, further along, close up against these grasses, stand the packed armies of mussels, fastened to the mud and grass by their dark threads.

Later on, when the impact of this morning's discoveries has lessened, I shall remember other flats I have known at low tide, each one holding its own especial character. I shall think of the stretching beach of Thumpertown, in Eastham, where the sand is clean and the water clear, and there is none of the mud of my own Wellfleet bay. The tide recedes at Thumpertown in parallel layers, so that, looking from the level of the dunes above the beach, there is a pattern of horizontal bands of pale, warm fawn and deep lilac where the drying sand meets the shallow water. You must wade over a quarter of a mile across these alternating bands of water and sand before you can reach the solid water of the bay. Standing in the rippling stretches of water, with the shifting shapes of the bright gold of sun-glint on its surface, you look down upon red-brown seaweed, waving beneath the wind-stirred sea like swaying ferns.

It is rich, varied, and beautiful, this world of the flats, this low-tide country of sand and mud. It may lack the dramatic violence of the Atlantic, but if you look closely at it, and stand still and listen, it will disclose immeasurable magic.

Trolling for the Bluefish

No, I told him, I have never fished before—that is, not with the rod. I have been out with the fishermen in the Mediterranean, laying our nets at midnight, sleeping then upon a bed of sailcloth for the three hours before dawn, when, with the first pale green light in the summer sky we drew in the nets. It was an exotic sea harvest, composed of bright-colored, elaborate-shaped fish: the fish for bouillabaisse. I knew that for a fact, for around five-thirty each morning we anchored the little boat against one of the islands and Jean Britinel, the skipper, helped me wade ashore. He kept a big kettle on that miniature island, at this particular point of landing. He had his supply of saffron and fresh water. We breakfasted on bouillabaisse made from the pick of the night's catch.

Perhaps I have instilled a false sense of magic into these recollections—that particular patina of magic acquired from the past. But I believe not. Every ingredient for bewitchment was there: the sea, the fishing, the light of summer dawn. Even the exciting element of tiny islands existed—for islands always hold enchantment.

My friend was listening. At first I feared he was disappointed, supposing me to be a mere romantic. But he was thinking.

"You're all right," he said slowly. "You're one of us. But you have a lot to learn. I can show you something you have never yet known. All you did out there in the Mediterranean was to wait while the fish swam into the nets. I can take you out here—and you'll get your islands, if you want them, just as wonderful as the ones you knew—and you can use your skill. You needed no skill over there. You relied merely upon chance and luck."

"Then you really will take me with you?" I asked.

I wanted to learn why fishing held such power over a man. It was something I did not yet understand. Never had I belonged to the fellowship of fishermen.

"Yes," he answered me. "Yes, of course we will take you. But, as I said before, you'll have to be content to learn."

Seriously we prepared for this fishing trip, assembling everything that might possibly be needed, from clam rakes and baskets to gunny sacks for the fish, first-aid kit, water bottles, sandwiches, bacon rind and eel skins for bait, and, of course, the clean-shaped rods with their nylon threads and the little teasing feathery minnowlike metal fish at the end; their eyes gleamed pink above the betraying hooks.

Below the sand dunes, far out over the flats, the little powerboat lay anchored. We waited for the turn of the tide. As the water floated the rowboat at the edge of the shore, we climbed down the dunes, laden with life belts and gear, and waded to the boat that was to take us out to the fishing craft.

58

And then I felt again the beauty of the sound and the movement of oars as I watched the gentle shape of our wake upon the smooth water. I would have been content just to sit in this little rowboat all the day long upon the surface of the bay. Already I had forgotten my urge to fish and betrayed the fact that I was no fisherman.

But our skipper glowed with the thought of today's fishing. For him there was no time to waste.

He marshaled us onto the powerboat. We pumped to bale the boat. It started with a roar. It speeded up, taking us out beyond the harbor and into the bay, gashing like scissors through the pale blue satin of the sea. And as we tore through the water it parted before us in glistening, white, sparkling spray. The wake stretched far behind us, heaving in a symmetrical pattern, dark at its center with undulating white foam fanning out at the sides; little boats tossed in the curl of its upheaval and swimmers back near the shore line felt the swell.

And now I saw this land as I had never seen it before. The sea that day was so smooth that it reflected the sand dunes upon its surface, a yellowish tinge. As I looked at it I realized that one does not truly know a land until one has seen it from the water.

"So that's how the bay joins the point of Indian Neck," I thought. "And neither, until this moment, did I realize that Blackfish Creek was so near."

In this era of flying, when the map of the land can be seen at a glance, and even the varying depths of the water are evident from the sky so that we know where the rocks lie beneath the sea and understand the gradual emergence of the land from the water, we might suppose we know everything about the formation of our earth. But there is an impersonal, superior view from the air, lacking the warm humanness of an approach from the sea.

59

There are two distinct experiences: sailing away from the country in which one lives, and arriving for the first time at a new land, from the sea. Some of my moments of greatest excitement have come out of sailing from a land, or arriving there. I saw myself as a child, nearing St. Malo, in Brittany, on my first Channel crossing. Those land sounds and land scents remain clear in my memory. And I thought then of a return to England after my first stay in America; a rooster crowed near Plymouth, and the sound rippled across the water to the ship, to be heard above the throb of the engines and the clatter of the life around me. And with the sound of this English rooster came a warm softness in the air and the scent of earth. This scent of earth is something very real. I have been aware of the scent of Sable Island from the deck of a transatlantic liner, while we were far out at sea beyond sight of land. It is as though water is an intensifier of the senses, for odors and sounds seem both, then, to have an emphasized clarity that is lacking when we are on shore.

Later today we shall return and land again, I promised myself. And I shall get the special thrill of coming nearer and nearer to shore. Magically that blur of blue will change and become landmarks I know. They may lose their mystery, but they will grow recognizable and friendly. And I shall smell the sun-warmed pines of the Cape, and the bayberry and the sweet fern, way out at sea.

While I was withdrawn into all this dreaming, the skipper had handed us the rods. We let out our lines, sitting in the stern of the boat. The lines dragged behind us, but an hour passed and nothing would strike.

I suppose I was impatient. I had expected the fish to strike the whole time.

"Are they always as scarce as this?" I whispered timidly to my neighbor, a hardened fisherman.

"It all depends," he answered. "But don't say anything. The doctor's getting to wonder, himself."

We looked for birds, but could see none. We went further out, beyond the submerged island of Billingsgate, around towards the tip of Great Island and Jeremy's Point.

And there we came across gulls and terns. In uncountable numbers they dipped and rose, circled and mewed. The water was so smooth that the white forms were reflected upon its surface, till we scarcely knew what we looked upon in this beautiful confusion of pattern. A dipper duck floated upon the water in front of the boat. And to our right, on the low sand of the tip of the island, we saw four wild duck, and swarms of black-headed sandpipers.

"Now we're in luck," said the doctor. "Always look for the birds and you'll know where to find the fish."

The sun burned down upon us. We were hot. And there, just before us, lay the point of the island. With one thought in our minds we looked at each other.

"Yes," decided our skipper. "We'll drop anchor and have a swim."

Diving off a small boat and swimming ashore: it is such things as this that restore enchantment, simple things that we ought to accept as the normal. The feel of deep water gives way to the shallow shore, then to the drag of the feet upon the sand, and at last to the wading to dry land. There were no waves. The water was transparent. Tiny fishes swam in their drilled shoals, doubled in the shadows they cast beneath them so that two shoals swam, one of fishes and the other of shadows, exact in shape and duplicating each movement. The sea seemed to melt into the sand at the shore, so gradual was the slope.

To walk from wet sand to dry sand, sand hot in the August sun, sand that burns the soles of the feet; and then, searching for shells and, after raising the little black-headed sandpipers who appeared to own this spit of land, to dive back into the water: the day was yielding great delight.

Around us now were other fishing boats, following the gulls. We passed one vessel, dragging for pogies.

We cut through calm water, our lines out beyond the stern of the little boat. But we had no strikes.

"It's a bad year for fishing," called the doctor, "though some days we have been catching around thirty bluefish. They just don't bite. There aren't even many stripers, although they say the ones that are caught come big this year. But the bluefish is elusive. That's what makes him such good sport to catch. Sometimes there are huge schools of them, and the bait passes among them and they won't turn a head. I don't know why, and neither does any honest fisherman. And you'll never catch me 'chumming.' Not on your life."

"But what's 'chumming'?" I asked, knowing I betrayed my ignorance.

"Oh," he answered, "that's when people have no sense of sportsmanship. They are so anxious to get their fish that they toss food upon the water to attract their attention. But not I. I'd rather come back at the end of a day with no catch at all."

His wife sighed.

"And I've got a fish fry planned for tonight," she said. "It looks as though I'll have to go to town and buy butterfish and clams."

We were passing through waters thick with seaweed. It deepened the sea to wine, and then dulled it to a heavy yellowish green. From time to time the rod bent and we imagined we had a strike, and there would be the excited whirr of the winding-in of the line; but always we found at the end of the line, entangled in the feathery lure and the bacon-rind bait, a humiliating cluster of seaweed.

62

I grew to mistrust this bending of the rod so that, when suddenly, after so many of these false hopes, I felt a convulsive shudder at the end of my line, for one fraction of a second I dared not believe my luck. But this time there was no doubt.

"Strike," I shouted, as I had been instructed to do, and the skipper slowed down the engine while I brought my rod around to the side of the boat and wound in like fury.

What will it be? Oh, what will it be? I thought. I almost trembled with excitement in my first catch. There was scarcely any weight at the end of my line, for the fish was swimming with the boat. Suppose there's nothing, after all? But again I felt the tug and I knew that it must be there.

It neared the boat. It dragged on the surface of the water: a beauty of a bluefish, weighing about three pounds. I whisked it over into the boat, where it wriggled. Watching it, I began almost to wish I had not caught it. One of the crew stabbed it with the knife and undid the hook. It lay there, subsiding, on the deck, panting and writhing till life ebbed from it. The last I saw of it, as I grew more and more ashamed of having robbed it of its life, was when some one put it into the empty gunny sack and laid it in water.

And then we wandered over this sea, so smooth that it was hard to imagine it as a force for danger. The low-flying gulls were doubled in the water. Lethargy enfolded us—a blue and silver lethargy. And then, into the blue and silver, with shimmers of gold from the sky, into this came a deep pink band: a band of fog towards Provincetown.

"Better watch out for that," said the skipper. "There's no knowing when it may roll in. Ever been at sea in a fog?"

Ever been at sea in a fog? I was in the middle of the Atlantic one winter day, enclosed in a fog thick like cream-colored flannel, with the mournful moan of the foghorn, and a sense of terror and desolation. It made no difference to this terror that I was one of many hundreds in this liner. The desolation was magnified those many times, as each one of us felt ourselves to be lost. I looked towards the pink band of fog, far out against Provincetown, and fear, like a serpent, crept into my serenity and my delight.

But the fog did not seem to draw any nearer. Neither did we catch another bluefish, though the surface of the water was splattered with little circles, like raindrops, where the minnows had been driven up by the fish.

"There must be swarms of them down there," sighed the doctor. "But they don't bite today."

At last we admitted defeat. It was agreed that I just happened to have had beginner's luck. We reeled in our lines and raced back to shore, the foam glistening around us like rubies and emeralds and diamonds as it caught the light of the afternoon sun. The waiting rowboat was, now at high tide, way out in deep water.

We cast the anchor of the fishing craft and, in a dim, exhausted way, transferred everything to the rowboat and made for shore.

"Well," said the doctor, as we climbed the dunes to his home. "If anyone were going to catch a bluefish I'm glad it was you. Perhaps now you'll come again one day soon, and—who knows?— maybe we'll get them by the score?"

That's it, I smiled to myself. It's the gamble. Perhaps next time?

The fish fry was a success, though we said nothing to the guests about having had to purchase the butterfish and clams. Just as I was leaving, my fisherman friend beckoned me to the kitchen.

"Look," he said. "You thought you were eating your fish—the fish you caught—didn't you? You thought it was in with all the rest of the fish we had to buy? Not a bit of it. I've got it safely here, and now, with you, I am going to clean it and fillet it, and you are

64

taking it back home with you tonight. It will taste good for your breakfast tomorrow—better than any fish you have ever eaten."

As I watched him clean and fillet my little fish, with all the precision of a surgeon, a strange sadness came over me. This bluefish was the deadest thing I had ever known. Its beauty had lain in its movement and its aliveness. I thought of the way the sun had caught the glisten of the scales. I remembered the wriggle and twist of the tail, the fury with which it had fought for its life. And in with this I remembered silver and blue, a satin-smooth sea and the sun beating down upon a little boat.

"It's been a wonderful day and I thank you for it," I told him. "And not only that, but now that I've caught a fish I feel that at last I belong."

Next morning, however, when I took the pallid little fillets out of the icebox I could scarcely bring myself to look at them. And when I had cooked them I could scarcely eat them. And when I ate them it was from a sense of duty.

"The poor fish," I found myself saying sentimentally. "The poor little fish. It had once been so beautiful."

Perhaps I am not meant to be a fisherman, after all.

Cranberries

The bogs look undramatic and far from interesting if you see them from some way off. They are flat stretches of land, intersected by the patterning of irrigation ditches. The vines grow thick and low upon the ground, and only when you look at them closely do you notice the beautiful delicate shape of their miniature leaves. Even at the height of their beauty—in the season of their blooming—you must come near to them to learn what they are really like. The blossom of the cranberry is fantastically tiny. But it is exquisite and involved in form, like a microscopic tiger lily. Some say it looks like a crane's head and neck, and that this was the reason for the name cranberry, which had started out as craneberry. It is delicate pale pink in color, but so frail and elusive that unless you are close to the bogs you are not even aware that the vines are in bloom. It seems, from the elaborate design of the little blossom, as though it should by rights be a very large flower; and you begin almost to wonder if something may not have happened to your own proportions: perhaps, unawares, you have grown suddenly into a giant, looking down upon a miniature world. So small a flower could surely have been simpler of form.

The blossom must be very sweet with honey, for in early summer, when the bogs are in bloom, the air is filled with a gentle booming hum and quivers with the movement of bees. I know this for a fact because one day when I was picking a little flower, in order to look at it more carefully, my feet were surrounded by bees and one of them, getting imprisoned between the sole of my foot and my sandal, most viciously stung me.

The cranberries themselves swell very rapidly. Scarcely have the petals fallen but the heavy, hard, green berries are hanging their heads on the frail stalks—those stalks which never seem as though they were strong enough to bear the weight.

This is distinctly a Cape Cod industry. The cranberry thrives on peat or muck land, loving the inevitable swamping of sand around its roots. It appears to have been in existence, in a primitive form, back across the centuries. The early Plymouth settlers are said to have found the wild cranberry, and it was voted by Provincetown, in 1773, that "any person should be found getting cranberrys before ye twentyeth of September exceeding one quart should be liable to pay one dollar and have the berys taken away."

Summer passes, and the green of the cranberry turns to red. Soon it will be the time to harvest.

And then, one morning as you walk near the bogs, you see the first signs of the gathering. Wooden boxes are piled upon the enfolding banks. They look strangely alien and out of place in this desolate setting, abrupt and naked against the softness of the undergrowth. Any day, we know now, the hordes will appear.

The sun has dried the dampness of early dew from the vines, as the harvesters arrive. They are like human locusts in the way they strip the bog. They gather the berries in a frenzy of attack, for these itinerant pickers are paid by the box, and they intend to earn as much as they can. They know that with true skill they are able, each one of them, to harvest fully eighteen to twenty barrels a day. Theirs is no attitude of sentiment. They are attuned to pillage.

The bog which, up to this moment, had been the most silent and deserted of places, has become, now, a confusion of movement and sound.

Nobody yet seems to have been able satisfactorily to mechanize the cranberry picking. Probably, one day soon, we shall see adequate machines supplanting the labor of these men, even as the mechanical picker is ousting the human cotton gatherer in the South. But for the present the cranberry is harvested almost entirely by hand, and even the scoop has changed little in design over the years. The same wooden scoop combs the bogs, though once it had a long handle, like a broom, and once, before that, it had a kind of clipper, like a pair of shears. Today it is broader and more shallow, and the score or more wooden teeth, made of the best rock maple, gleam with a polish acquired as the teeth are drawn through the waxy leaves and stems of the cranberry. But the principle of the scoop remains the same, determined by experience.

And now the harvesters creep across the bog upon their knees, with a sense of order despite the apparent commotion. They are strung out along one width of the bog, and as they comb the cranberries into the wooden scoops they make a beautiful fanlike shape before them, to right and to left, with a swaying movement. I feel I am watching the figure of a ballet, there is such rhythm in their harvesting gestures.

And perhaps there is an additional rhythm because the pickers are Portuguese. Against this New England landscape they seem strangely exotic. The dark-skinned, lean bodies hold a Latin grace that is lacking in the Anglo Saxon. Sprinkled in with the Portuguese, and looking, if possible, even more alien to our northern Cape Cod, are the yet darker-skinned Bravas—the half-negro, half-Portuguese, who have come from Cape Verde to settle in certain parts of the upper Cape. The only true New Englander is the overseer, standing on the bank as he directs the workers. Contrasted with the innate rhythm in the bodies of the pickers, his movements seem discordantly angular and rigid.

The pickers rock their scoops, filling them with crimson cranberries. They empty them into waiting boxes, and, louder than the steady background swish of the scoops against the waxy plants or the rustle of the harvesters as they move across the bog upon their knees, loud and brittle comes the sound of the cranberries, falling like hail into the wooden boxes.

Watching them as they creep over the bog, once more I am sadly conscious of a sense of emotional detachment about this harvesting. These people who have not tended the vines over the year can never be expected to feel love for the berries they comb into the scoops. And thus there is no joy. Neither is there much spirit of teamwork. Irked by the monotony of his job, each man harvests for himself, the sole feeling of community lying in resentful boredom. It is a boredom that causes the muscles of the body to sag by midday, the hand to numb and the mind to get dulled. Up and down rocks the scoop, to right and to left; and the only possible variety is a vague comparison between the well-weeded, rich picking of one bog and the poison-ivy-encumbered, leaner harvesting of another.

But in the background, wise enough to stay remote from the crew he has hired, wandering on the far edge of the bordering

70

banks is old Ezra Newcomb, who owns these bogs and loves them. Today he is an outcast, though it is his cranberries that they pillage.

As he looks at the impersonal scene before him, watching as Portuguese and Bravas bring the cranberries ashore, he relives the months of work and worry that have culminated in this harvesting. He remembers that time when the blunt-nosed leaf hoppers brought the disastrous virus of false blossom to the bogs. Sweeping his insect net back and forth across the vines—over the Early Blacks and the Howes—trembling with anxiety as to how many of the hoppers he would take in the net, he had realized the extent of the infestation. And he recollects the pathetic way in which the diseased little blossoms stood erect upon the stalk, instead of being turned downwards, as was their healthy wont. Fruitworm and gypsy moth, root grub, girdler and fire beetle, bagworm and scale: there seemed no end to the countless insects whose purpose in life was to destroy his vines. And, as if this were not enough, he had also to give hostage to the elements, with their power of winter-killing and drought.

He sees his bogs, now, warmed by the sun, glowing with the ripe red cranberries, and he knows that his harvest is the result of exact knowledge of the moment for holding the winterflood and for draining the bogs. And as he watches the gatherers creeping over the vines with their scoops, old Ezra Newcomb remembers his excitement when science and progress had come to his aid and the magical helicopter had hovered in the sky above his land, spraying and dusting against insect pests.

The love he holds for his cranberry bogs is the outgrowth of the trouble and anxiety they have given him.

When the last scoop has been emptied into the last box and the harvest is piled high in the little gray-shingled packing house at the end of the main bog, quietness will return to his vines. Impatiently he awaits this moment, for something within him resents this alien invasion, even while he admits to its inevitability. And he will rejoice when the final vestiges of the gathering have disappeared and the barrels are despatched to the screen house.

Then he will be able to look at his bogs and not feel that he is betraying them. Soon, with the first touch of frost upon the myriad tiny leaves, he will see the vines turn to the color of wine, and the countryside will become like lakes of this purple wine. They will stay thus, giving beauty to the landscape, until the moment comes for the flooding of the bogs. He will set the pumping plants in motion and the water will rush into the irrigation ditches. Within a few hours it will overflow the ditches, and flood the bogs themselves. And they will be like sudden, man-made ponds, protecting the cranberry plants against the assault of frost and winterkill, and the attack of scale and the red mite.

If you should come to Cape Cod in the winter, having known this part of the world only in summertime, you would be confused at the change in the landscape. The cranberry bog is normally unobtrusive, never asserting itself but stretching there on the flat land in the sandy acid soil upon which it thrives. Drive by and you will scarcely notice it. But early in the year, while the Cape is still deserted, you will suddenly see numberless ponds that had never before existed. There are chains of ponds, and severely rectangular ponds, and little ponds standing alone. On a bright sunshiny day they reflect the sky, till between the blue above and the purple-crimson of the submerged bog, they give off an irridescent purplish blue. If you chanced to stop and look closely at them, you would see that the ponds are fringed with crimson, overlooked, unharvested cranberries that have risen to the surface of the water and drifted with the wind to the edges of the bogs. Sometimes these have been raked and scooped up, and then you will notice them,

72

swollen from their months in the water, heaped upon the banks in beautiful but useless piles.

But, too, you should not forget to look down into the depths of these ponds, for there, protected by the flowage, lie the cranberry plants in all their loveliness, purple still, but waiting for next year's budding.

The Scents
of Cape Cod

History says that Napoleon always knew when he was nearing his native island of Corsica, even while he was still far out at sea, by the scent of the maquis wafted to his ship by the wind.

I can believe this, for I have smelt the maquis of Corsica—this sweet-scented undergrowth of pale mauve bushes of blossoming rosemary and myrtle and herbs.

I like to think that in the same way I could tell when I was nearing Cape Cod, were I at sea in the Atlantic Ocean. For the Cape has its own special Northern scents, and it is through these that most intensely I remember it.

Cape Cod scents are many. Some of them continue throughout the year, while others appear suddenly, in due season.

If you are fortunate, on any return to the Cape after an absence, you will pass South Wellfleet at low tide. Drive along the highway then, and the first impact of the Cape reaches you.

"We're here," we shout. "We're here at last."

And the realization comes to us, not through our eyes, looking across the marshes to the shining bay and our first sight of water, but through our sense of smell. For over those marshes, even into the car that speeds along the highway, over that expanse of low-lying land comes the scent of the tidal mud of Cape Cod.

I suppose you might call it an objectionable odor. If we insulated it from its associations we would be conscious of a heavy, decaying, almost sulphurous scent. It was this same low-tide scent that I noticed when I watched the dredging of Wellfleet harbor. It came from the exposed mud that had lain on the bed of the bay over the years, deep beneath the purifying contact with oxygen and light. But now, each time we return to the Cape, this smell means happiness. It heralds days of sunlight, and silver days at sea.

There are scents that mark the passing of the months and the rhythm of the year. Rarely do the summer visitors arrive early enough to meet the honey locusts in bloom. The Cape then is milky white with the blossom. It is like a film across the land, loud even into late evening with the hum of bees. Thick over the countryside floats the sickly sweet scent of the locust.

This happens before the sun has strength enough to draw the resinous odor from the pines. It is as though the year spaces its perfumes, lest we should have any moment when we are not satisfied and delighted. For, when summer is in high fling, the sun-touched pine trunks exude a warm sweet odor, till each one of us is drawn to some special place where we have smelled it before, knowing that the power of scent tosses us backwards in time. In my own memory I return to the Mediterranean; but then I laugh as I tell myself that it is no longer only the Mediterranean. These days it is Cape Cod. For Cape Cod has overlaid my European past. And why, when I sit at the edge of a pond here near Wellfleet, should I feel a need to think of wandering on the shores in the South of France? But the nostalgic power of this sense of smell is so strong that it seems as though one must gather up to oneself all possible memories, from way back and far away. The actual present is not enough.

Into this resinous odor there creeps another scent. The white sand paths through the woods, and the lanes that bind one part of the Cape to another, are fringed with sweet fern. Perhaps, of all these scents, this is the one that, to me, though I know it is found all over northern New England, most completely belongs to Cape Cod. If you want to feel yourself into the mood of the Cape, you should pull leaves from this beautiful fringed plant, shaped like the elongated doodling of green fingers, as you walk, and crush them to sniff the perfume. Sentimentally I have picked these leaves and kept them, dried and pressed in a book, so that I might smell them through the months of winter. It is a rough, robust scent, belonging to salt and sea.

And then if we leave the sand paths and the woods, and go to the open moors on the back road to Truro, we find them covered with bay. Silvered in late summer with their clusters of berries, the bay bushes have leaves that smell like the scented myrtle of the Mediterranean. And when I pick some of these leaves, warmed by the sun, I remember a fishing village in Majorca, where on festival days the peasants would strew the street with sprays of this myrtle. As we trod upon the carpet of green, crushing the leaves beneath our feet, a scent rose high into the air, stronger even than the incense from the swung censers. I like to imagine how it would be if we, up here in the North, were to do the same. A carpet of

77

sweet fern and bay would smell good, under a hot summer sky.

There is one scent that I miss on the actual Cape. I wonder how many people have been lucky enough to visit Martha's Vineyard at the exact moment when the wild grape is in bloom? That peculiarly insignificant little flower is generally overlooked because of interest in the grape itself. It has no brilliance of color with which to proclaim its existence. It clumps there, in the shadow of the swelling vine leaves, a pale yellow-green cluster of misty bloom. But go to the high dunes of Gay Head on the Vineyard, around the early part of July, and you will smell upon the air, even above the scent of the sea or the perfume of abounding wild roses, the elusive perfume that gives its name to Martha's Vineyard: it is the scent of the wild grape.

The same wild roses are to be found here on the Cape, too. Thoreau, in his book on Cape Cod, grew ecstatic about these roses that grow on the sandy stretches in such profusion that, at the time of their blooming, it is like a pink carpet covering the land.

"No Italian or other artificial rose-garden could equal them," he wrote. "They were perfectly Elysian, and realized my idea of an oasis in the desert."

I believe there must be something in sea air that gives such special scent to these wild roses. It may merely be that the air itself is so particularly clear that all scents hold additional strength. But I do know that never, anywhere, have I smelled such magic of perfume as comes from this spread of pink roses between Wellfleet and Truro, on the way to Bound Brook Island, or on the back road between South Wellfleet and Orleans. And the deep pink color of these roses—a purity of color that makes one think of the cotton frocks of young girls—is a fit counterpart to their scent. It has a clean, rain-washed quality.

I know one rosebush here on the Cape that especially I love. It

78

often seems to me that we humans are incapable of loving in general, and on principle. We need and seek some one small thing that is intimate and close. We cannot truly love the Grand Canyon as we can love with understanding a particular flower in our own back yard. When I think of the roses on Cape Cod, I think of a bush that grows out of the very sand itself. Nourished by sand and salt air, it yet thrives and blooms with grandeur. It is not a pink rose, but one of the few single white roses that we find in this part of the land, with an extravagant number of thorns and prickles. Here in Wellfleet it is called the Franklin rose, and legend tells that it was washed ashore and took root about a century ago when a ship called the *Franklin*, laden with plants and seeds, was wrecked off the back shore at Newcomb's Hollow. If the scent of a flower can be said to symbolize exquisite purity, that of this white rose does so. I visit it each summer, to watch for the first opening bud. It grows in a sheltered valley of sand, tucked into the high cliffs that overhang the Atlantic Ocean. If the legend is a true one, the wind that day must have been fierce, to toss the plant to the top of those cliffs. But here it stands, so close to the ocean that, at the moment of a high course tide, in the fall or the early spring, were its petals at that time of year in existence you could gather them into your hand and fling them from the cliff into the ocean.

Once the wild roses have blossomed and faded, we feel that summer is richly with us. The perfumes of the young year have gone, taking with the roses the strong sweet scent of the wild white azalea that has been growing high in the hedgerows. Soon, as the sun gets more fierce, we shall seek with a sense of relief those things that speak to us of cool water and shade. And so, as the month of July passes, I turn to the water lilies on the ponds.

Many people would say that the water lily is beautiful to look upon, but that it has no scent. And they might be right, if they demanded an obvious perfume. But, should you gather some pond lily buds and, placing them in a shallow bowl, smell them as they open in the early morning, you would know that they hold a perfume that is as exquisite as it is indefinable. The only way I can describe this scent is to say that it is like the taste of anis in a drink of absinthe in France; it has a strange, cold, watery, almost malign perfume.

Summer passes, and the next scent that I seek brings with it a sting of thin sadness, for it signals the turn of the year. It is the end of July, and blueberry-picking season. Blossoms everywhere are changing to fruit. The little green cranberry in the bogs has started to flush orange and then pale red. And now, at this late moment, the sweet pepper bush comes into flower. At the edges of the smaller ponds and the disused cranberry bogs, the bushes grow thick and tall, loving moist sand around their roots. This white spire of blossom, the clethra as it should be called, is a lure to the bees. They boom among the delicate blooms, making from them a special, very pale honey. The scent of this flower has a Northern purity, white in quality as the actual color of the blossom itself.

And so it runs, this rhythm of a year of perfumes. But the patterns of seasonal perfumes are threaded into the permanent scents of the Cape itself. These are composed of fish and tar, rope, seaweed and salt air, the quality of a clear morning after a northeaster, or the particular smell of low tide. And these endure, come summer, come winter, sun or storm, the essence of a sea-girt land.

Lighthouses

It is difficult to be coldly factual in thinking of lighthouses. Something about them makes one feel romantic, and even sentimental. They are needed symbols and visible tokens of safety and strength. The element of nostalgia seems always to surround them, for each one of us—if we are fortunate—holds the memory of some particular lighthouse from childhood days.

My own special memory goes back to England. I lived near a lighthouse on the shores of the North Sea. As I lay in bed in the night nursery, I watched the light. First it stroked the picture of a hunting scene on the far wall, then the top corner of the wardrobe, then the foot of the bed itself, over and over again. From the regular flash of this light came my first conscious awareness of the passage of time. But when winter brought the gales and the sea was rough, I grew distressed by the recurrent flash. Lying warm and safe in my bed, I thought of the fishermen upon the sea, guided by this light. And I would get out of the warm bed and kneel before the nursery window, in the cold, to watch the lighthouse beams stroking the stormy sea.

Once each year, in my childhood, our father took us to visit the lighthouse. Up uncountable steps, breathless from the effort, to the very top we climbed. And there, in a magical, frightening world of prisms and glass, Father and the keeper would explain the working of the light. We grew up with a sense of respectful awe for lighthouses.

And so it is that I shall always look upon them as things you climb, things with uncountable steps that finally reach to the very top. But I shall never be able to get accustomed to modern mechanization. For a lighthouse should have a keeper. And the keeper should be a warm, fatherly man who is kind to little children and lets them wander around and even climb to the very top of his lighthouse. Everything associated with it should be benign; for is it not, after all, the symbol of support and strength?

Something sad has happened. The warm, human quality has gone forever from the lighthouse. Today it is completely impersonal, even as it is mechanically perfect. Automatically, on the dot of sunset, though the sky may still be bright, punctually, at the precise minute of the official setting of the sun, a button is pressed by remote control and the light comes on.

But something even worse has taken place. Fear and suspicion have invaded our lives. You are forbidden to enter the lighthouse. Never again can you climb to the very top. The authorities, reacting to the prevailing temper of our times, are afraid of sabotage.

82

With this new order, a sense of frustration enters the spirit, robbing the lighthouse of the completely friendly quality which used always to exist. And this quality is something we need. For our lighthouses satisfy some deep, unformulated hunger of the human spirit. They represent more than their basic functioning. They are part of our faith and our religion.

One of the most important lighthouses on the Atlantic forbids you even to wander upon the grounds surrounding it. It has assumed the quality of a prison. Over many years I walked there, out to the edge of the high cliffs, loving the beauty of the tower in varying lights. But suddenly, today, you may not do so.

You can walk around the rope that has been strung along the edge of the cliff. And, if I am to be objectively honest, I must admit that one can see almost as much this way as one used to. But the very existence of that rope puts a crimp into the freedom of the human soul.

Recently—though I have shrunk from visiting it since the era of suspicion clamped down upon us—I went to this particular lighthouse on an evening in early fall. The sun set in fantastic colors. The ocean was pale green, and smooth as velvet. Over the sea, the sky at this sunset hour glowed lilac and pink. The whole world seemed unbelievably lovely, except for that forbidding sign: No Trespassers. Keep Out. Why did they have to feel such fears? I wondered.

And then, perfect in its timing, at that moment of my hurt questioning, I heard a warm, human voice.

A young coastguardman sat at the open window of the Coast Guard station attached to the lighthouse, telephoning to his girl. It was Saturday evening. Across the still air, as I sat in the car, reluctant to venture near this forbidden territory, I heard him as he talked: "Baby," he was saying, unaware that I could hear, "are you there, sweetheart? Is that you? Listen, baby, I'll let you know when I can get off."

The talk ambled on, filled with such sweet intimacies that I was almost ashamed of listening. But I needed this reassurance. I had been reminded that it takes more than this impersonal, technological perfection to subdue the human heart. Delighting in the conversation, I stayed there, treacherously hidden within my car, in the deepening dusk.

But nothing could destroy the beauty of the lighthouse itself rising high into the sky. I watched it there, before me, as the sun set and dusk covered the land.

I watched it change color. The lantern—that glass enclosure around the prisms—hardly showed, as yet, in the lingering light of evening. But, against the steel blue of the Atlantic, just after the setting of the sun, the white pillar of the lighthouse had turned pale pink like a fondant in a candy store. And then, by contrast, the light within the lantern became a strangely cold, dim green. I walked round to the far side, upon the edge of the cliffs, to see the lighthouse silhouetted against the sunset over the bay. From here, as I looked back towards it, I saw it deep violet upon the blazing orange of the sky.

And then, as the minutes passed, the light grew brighter with the fading glow in the sky till already it began noticeably to stroke the radar pylons that stand against the station.

I watched the prisms revolve. Soon, I knew, the pillar of the lighthouse would grow insubstantial, and merge into the dusk. Silence was around me, broken only by the evening twitter of birds, nesting in the clay pounds of the cliffs. But the glow from the western sky still held the power to fire the windows of the Coast Guard buildings till they flamed in squares of gold.

All color had gone now from the land. The burnt crimson of

the fading huckleberry foliage had turned to black. The men's blue dungarees, hanging upon the clothesline at the back of the lighthouse, also were black. From the edge of the cliff, the white tower itself had become black. The desolate landscape had lost the sharpness of its edges. Suddenly it was growing cold, and the wind had risen, waving the grasses around me. And now for the first time the rays of the light were strongly visible, endlessly turning, stroking, flashing, through the hours of night until the exact moment of sunrise.

Looking up at the outside of this press-button lighthouse flanked by the radar pylons, I thought back to the days when the keeper had lit this light with a match. I saw him, shortly before sunset, climbing the circular iron stairway with the iron treads, up to the lantern at the top of the tower. It was whitewashed inside; always it had to be whitewashed. Every lighthouse I have known was whitewashed, back to childhood memories by the North Sea. Surely, too, it must have had that particular cold smell, mixed with the smell of metal polish and kerosene, that I remember so well.

I like to suppose that despite the endless repetition, day after day, year after year, the keeper must have had, each evening, a renewed feeling of awe, surmounting the mere sense of duty. For was it not he who guarded the flame? In his hands lay the safety of men and ships at sea. As he climbed those innumerable stairs to the top of the lighthouse, he knew that it was up to him to keep the seaways open and clear, all the way along the Atlantic Ocean, for the passage of the ships. Dulled by routine and the tedium of aloneness, he yet must have felt, always, a humble power. Far back into the days of whale oil, in the late seventeen hundreds, when this lighthouse was commissioned, his forebears must have felt it. Somewhere nearer in time, as the light was lit from a kerosene wick, this same feeling, surely, endured. And then, as the years passed, and the kerosene wick changed, with progress, to kerosene vapor, the keeper pumped the kerosene by hand from the pneumatic pump, so that the vapor went up the tube into the tower and into the Bunsen burner through jets: still it was a man who had to light it. Through these many years—when the carrying power of kerosene outrivaled today's electricity, so that the light could be seen for a full fifty miles at sea—through the years after the acetylene tanks had arrived, the keeper needed always to be there.

And then, only about five years ago, electricity took over. Man was suddenly of little importance. He could be dispensed with.

When they made the change in this lighthouse they tore down the lens and the three prisms, those exquisite works of art that had been brought over from Paris. They did not even save them for a museum, where by rights they belong. They chose to ignore their historical value, leaving the shattered glass lying around the base of the lighthouse for anyone to salvage. And away into oblivion went the beautiful light that had been worked by weights from the top of the tower to the bottom, like a gigantic grandfather's clock. Mercury-bearing, it had been, with three or four tons of this precious mercury, and so sensitive that it took only the lightest touch of a finger tip to make it function. You could get right inside the lens, it was so big.

The keeper would tell me with pride of the cleaning of the prisms.

"You had to draw the curtains all around you up there, in the glass lantern, when you cleaned the prisms during the daytime," he said. "You had to do this to prevent the sun from acting as a burning glass and setting everything on fire. And the sun would have cracked the lens, too, if the curtains were not drawn."

I remembered, then, having noticed these drawn curtains, on

some of my visits to the Light, and wondering about them.

They were always busy, these keepers, with their two assistants, cleaning and scrubbing and polishing the light, standing the four-hour watches, tending the fog signal in the brick house near the beach bank. And being busy they scarcely noticed the loneliness around them. This feeling of solitude was left to the womenfolk, living out there with their men on the bleak cliff, remote from all neighbors.

And something of this aloneness entered into the fiber of the keeper's children. I once knew the son of a lighthouse keeper. He carried within him a strange mixture of resentment and fear. It was the hardest thing in the world to get him to talk about his childhood, spent out there fantastically alone, on the sand cliffs of Cape Cod. Fired with a sense of the romance of such a life, I would try to draw him out, hoping to gain some insight into the essential elements of his childhood. Here should be a human being who had been kept remote from the cheapening qualities of the modern world, someone with that particular superawareness of the solitary. But no; his one aim and purpose in life had been to free himself of this ghastly monotony, this complete dearth of the unexpected, the utter choking of the sense of adventure.

"But didn't you share with your father that almost sacred feeling about the lighting of the light?" I asked him. "Didn't you feel awe and respect for the life he led?"

The grown-up son shrugged his shoulders.

"That was all right for my father," he answered. "All those feelings kept him going. Why, the light was so holy to him that he only let me go up into the lantern about once a year, as a special treat. . . ."

And so he ran away. He went to sea and became, later, a successful businessman in a city. Perhaps all sons of lighthouse keepers run away. That would be the inevitable swing of the pendulum of life.

There was one important concession, however, that this man made.

"I never would have admitted it while I was still young," he said. "But I'll tell you now. That life there, all alone by myself, running up and down the cliffs for sheer fun, walking around among the brids' nests in the clay pounds of the high cliffs, running along the beach, and even walking the miles to the village and back, over and over again, just on the chance of meeting some one, all this turned me inwards and brought out the dreamer in me. It gave me a sort of mystical unity with life which wasn't important those years while I was still a boy, but which came out and developed in me later on. Perhaps you'll laugh at me when I tell you that those early years did something to me. I hate them. I fear them. And I despise them. And nothing on earth will ever take me back to that Light, now it is all changed. I haven't even been there since my father died, no, not once. But something got born in me during those lonely years. I suppose the religious people and the psychiatrists would have names for it. I haven't. I only know that I grew to take for granted all sorts of things happening to me—things I saw, and heard, that no one else seemed to be able to see and hear. Why, I'd take it for granted that I had someone with me when I walked alone by myself on a winter day in a storm; and I *know* I had."

Suddenly he grew ashamed of his disclosures, and a fixed look came upon his face.

"But the main thing that happened to me," he went on in a much louder, more emphatic voice, "the main thing I gained from those terrible years alone there, as a child, with nothing but that light going round and round and round, night after night after

88

night, was a sense of strength. I learned the strength of rebellion, and nothing in the whole of God's earth can resist me in my fight."

That was it, I reflected. The light went round and round and round, and then again round and round and round. Over the nights, the weeks, the months, the years.

And now this human element has passed. The keeper and the struck match have made way for radio and radar and every possible contraption of modern science, so that many of our lighthouses are no longer needed. Some have fallen back into the earth itself. On the island of Billingsgate—where the sea has eroded the land so that, after having been once a village with dwellings and a school house, it is now nothing but a stretch of sand, evident only at low tide—over there, they tell me, once stood a lighthouse. And down along the shore line at Mayo's Beach, in Wellfleet, stood another lighthouse. This was a range one, shining only to sea, so that the ships far out in the bay could take their bearings from it. You can still see some of the foundations, and, next to this site, you will notice a two-storied, pointed-roofed house, which is where the lighthouse keeper and his family lived. Very often these have survived, and always they are of the same design, proclaiming the earlier existence of a lighthouse in the same way that you will see sudden clumps of lilac bushes and wizened apple trees—house spots, they call them, here on Cape Cod—growing still when the houses themselves have vanished.

Our lighthouses may have become impersonal, but at least they still exist, standing there against the skyline, overlooking the ocean. Should the time come when we no longer hold any need for them, let us hope that the human spirit will have developed in such a manner that it does not require the symbol of this tower of light, steadfast throughout all storms, stroking the night skies.

Fishing

The summer people have barely left Cape Cod when the fishermen come to town. And then the hotels are filled with great rubber boots hanging upside down in the lobby to dry. You can see the fishermen's cars all over the Cape; the roads and the beaches are filled with them. You know them, always, for they have rods fixed to the tops, rods sticking out behind, rods, it would seem, everywhere, at all angles. And now an entirely different mood invades these hotels. Nobody dresses for dinner in the early part of October. There is a cozy smell of steaming wool as soaked socks dry on the radiators. Thermos bottles stand around, waiting to be filled. The fishermen keep the strangest hours. After dinner, as they talk together of the day's luck, you will see them slip off to bed fantastically early, setting their alarm clocks to one in the morning, or two or three or four. For the impassioned fisherman's life is governed by the tides and the quarter of the wind.

The fishermen have taken possession. They dominate the town.

When I talk of fishermen I mean, at this moment, the top layer in the strict hierarchy of the fishing world: the surf casters. These are the men who wait the year round for the beginning of October, for the striped bass on their way south to the fresh-water rivers of Rhode Island, where they lie in the mud all winter till they are seined in early spring. These fishermen are the fanatics to whom perfection of casting is all important.

"Three hundred dollars' worth of tackle to get two fish—and the fish aren't tremendously good to eat when you've got them," cynically sneers a trout-fisher friend of mine, who lives on one of the ponds. "Never went much for bass fishing myself. Rather sit there in my boat in the middle of the pond and play my trout. These striper men stay out all the night long and go and get wringing wet and almost freeze to death—and for what?"

I notice with amusement—though I say nothing—that he has taken the trouble, all the same, to leave his pond and come along here to the back shore to look at the surf casters.

And it is most surely a beautiful sight.

The beach is fringed with fishermen. Standing there, hour after hour, at the water's rim or wading even into the surf itself, they are like an edging of pointed dark lace upon the foamy skirt of the ocean. I watch them as they cast, trying to grasp the essence of their movements. But it is always so rapid. Just when I am saying to myself, There, it's like that, they—— just then the entire rhythmic gesture has been fulfilled, and the lure lies out in the ocean two hundred or more feet from shore. Over and over again

I try to capture the action, to learn exactly wherein lies this beauty. My friend Howard, the trout fisherman, has met up with a surf-caster acquaintance, and now, knowing my concern, he is getting him to instruct me.

"The good caster makes use of his rod," the surfman tells me, delighted in talking about his artistry. "The correct caster *becomes* his rod. The flow of energy from his body goes into the rod. Look at the man over there—the one in the red shirt. He checks his backward movement like a spring coil. There's nothing abrupt. It's all smooth. That's good, and right. And then look at that other man—the far one down the shore. He just whips it, all stiff, and doesn't let it go the whole way back as he should. You'd be surprised at how many fishermen don't know how to cast. About sixty per cent of them, I'd say."

The light of fanaticism shines in his eyes.

But while I listen to him I find myself watching the men as they cast. The movements are so completely beautiful. One leg hangs loosely behind at the moment of the cast, at that moment when the body gives a lovely, subtle little twist. Why has no one thought of creating a ballet around the surf caster? A modern ballet, it should be, with the diagonals of the rods—the glass rods, the black-finish hollow Fiberglas rods, the split bamboo rods, the one-piece pure Calcutta bamboo rods—the lines of these rods obliquely across the scene, at all angles, straight, and then, at that magical split second of the cast, curved like a scimitar. All these straight lines, and curves, are set against the frilly background of the foamy edge to the sea, which is splashing their legs—soaking them till their waterproof boots turn dark, drenching them till their parkas get stained with the sea. The shapes of the breakers are dazzling white and frothy, like cauliflowers, against the shouting colors of some of the fishermen themselves, in their bright-red wool shirts.

"It is not really a day for the striper," says Howard's surfcaster acquaintance. "If the sea would only lie down a little the fish would be easier to catch. They get sand in their gills when it's rough; and they don't like that. They don't like it when the sand bars get kicked up by the wind, either."

Howard nods his head in agreement.

"I know," he answers. "And they feed on the little stars out there on the sand bars. They've got to be able to get at them."

It is late afternoon, and the dunes are in shadow. Purple shadows fling themselves further and further down, across the sand of the beach. A straight, thin line of birds flies along the water, only a little way out from shore.

"Look," says Howard, his eyes lighting up with pleasure. "Do you see them? Sea coot, they are, those with the white on them. And a few eider duck as well. But I bet you anything none of these surf casters will have noticed them. They're just fanatics, they are—not even aware of the gulls floating in the sky above us, with their beautiful set of wings. They don't know anything outside of the perfection of the cast."

I am finding myself involved in so many different attitudes of mind and values. It is as though I am living in three worlds, at one and the same time: I, myself, concerned with the sheer beauty of these human bodies, with the twist and turn, the fling and the recoil of the rod; my friend Howard watching and loving all the little creatures that wing their way across our path; and his acquaintance, thinking only of the striped bass that swim there, out of sight, ready for his plug or his jig.

"The gunners are after the sea coot," I hear Howard saying. "It's open season just now, so long as you shoot them in open water. And it's one of the very oldest sports, too, shooting sea coot. But it's silly, and wrong, for you can't eat them, and you can't

94

even get them when you've shot them, for they fall down into the water. I've seen the men sitting there in the bay, in two dories, popping them off. It's what I call a bad sport."

I hear him talking about the little white-marked sea coot, and at the same moment I hear the surf caster telling me more of the art of fishing.

"There are different schools of thought about surf casting," he goes on, while he stands there at the edge of the Atlantic Ocean, the end of his rod secured into the pocket of the leather girdle that he wears around his waist. "Some say one thing and some another. But I feel the only thing that really matters is to keep yourself loose in the cast, and to thumb your reel properly, so as to avoid backlashing. Eighteen inches between line and leader is what I stand for, seeing to it that the line is guided by the thumb as it comes off the spool——"

"Yes," automatically I agree, knowing that he has no possible awareness of the extent of my abysmal ignorance. "Yes," I repeat, "I know. I think you're right."

And all the time I am watching the rhythmic dignity of the fishermen along the shore. Were we to know the truth, they are probably obscure little accountants from New Jersey, or insecure, unimportant salesmen from the outskirts of Boston. But they have been ennobled by their attire so that I gaze upon warriors and knights.

That man over to my right: he stands up against the force of the whole of God's North Atlantic. Were we to inquire into his background we would find that he was, in the balance of today's reckoning, the essence of mediocrity. But look at him now as he wades into the encroaching surf.

These men do not stay at the hotels. We are in the ranks now of those who sleep overnight in their cars. Beach buggies, we call them, if we want to be completely dignified. The fat little man I am talking to at this moment, this strange, squat creature in the thick black-and-white-check coat, who has none of the look of the fisherman, is consumed with the same fanaticism, the crazy, inexplicable hunt for the striped bass here on Cape Cod. But what does he do over the rest of the year? He comes from Milton, or Lowell, or somewhere or other, just outside of Boston. Already I have forgotten which, for it is of little importance. And he has driven all through the night to get here to the Cape. And he's tired. He's dead, dog-tired, if you want to know the truth. And in a few moments he's going back to his ramshackle old car to curl up and sleep for a few hours, for the short time till dawn. But he stands here now in the cold water—dreadfully, piercingly cold, this late evening in October—casting for the striper. And he doesn't really know why he is doing this. Something drives him beyond his understanding.

Looking at him, standing so tired and cold and wet, I find my-self filled with a great tenderness. Is he, perhaps, running from something—some confusion of living that is overcoming him—as the colored people in North Carolina will escape from responsi-bilities, and go and sit on the banks of a muddy little creek, all the day long, a bamboo rod in their hands, and a worm at the end of their line of string, hoping a catfish might come their way? Is he infused with some longing for the perfection of pure craftman-ship? Or does he merely want to get away from his own narrow, nagging world, away from the womenfolk who surround him, and be alone under the sky?

Whatever may be their motive, these men hold tremendous beauty. There is something oddly medieval about their appear-ance. My mind keeps on returning to the Early Italian painters. Here are figures that Uccello or Piero della Francesca might have

98

painted, with the enormous loose boots turned down over their knees or drawn high to their waists, wrinkled and filled with rich folds and curves and bulges.

As dusk blurs the beach, the men are simplified yet more, standing there silhouetted in black against the pale green ocean. And with this simplification, they assume an even greater sense of majesty, till they become timeless, and belong to all the ages.

Night falls. I look at the surf casters, dim-edged now against the darkness, and I know that this same scene before me is to be found fringing the coastline of the Atlantic; on the rigidly straight banks of the Cape Cod Canal where, they say, three to four thousand fishermen can be counted during one night at the height of the season; and on the islands of Nantucket and Martha's Vineyard. Along the shore from Nova Scotia to Cape Fear, men are standing there, wet and cold, seeking the striped bass. They sleep in their cars, enduring discomfort that they would resist and reject, were it imposed upon them. They may, or they may not, catch a striper. But that is not of paramount importance.

Thinking of the actual stripers, I walk down the beach to see who has had any luck. And I stop and talk to a man. He isn't much of a fisherman, really. But the flame consumes him.

"I've been watching you," he says, as I pause, "watching you coming down the beach. And I though I'd ask you: Have they caught anything up there? We have to listen hard, you see, to find from the other fellows where the fish are running. I aim to go up to Nauset tomorrow if I have no luck here. I'm about done in, now, at this moment. Drove all night to get here. I'm just about to go and curl up in my beach buggy—that's mine, over there, at the far end, if you can still see it—and have a sleep."

The beach, so empty now of summer visitors, is riddled with the deep tracks of the beach buggies. Great wheel-curves cover the sand, and into these curves are woven the patterns of the large flat feet of the fishermen, in their enormous rubber boots, and the frail, beautiful hieroglyphs of the feet of the gulls and terns, delicate against the monumental imprints of the fishermen's boots.

"Did you find anyone who'd caught anything?" he repeats, anxiously.

"Only one," I tell him with reluctance. "Just one. And it wasn't even a striper. It was merely a large blue."

I leave them as they stand there, endlessly casting, casting, casting. But, as I drive back to town I find myself remembering the one dramatic catch of the year. It held none of the snobbishness of so much surf casting. The fisherman was merely a youngster who spent his vacations on the Cape.

He was the buddy of my young neighbor friend, Tom.

I chanced to be there, actually on the spot, when he got his striper. It happened the very night before the boy was leaving Cape Cod.

We were on the back shore, in August. Suddenly we saw a crazy school of stripers. They were jumping clean out of the water, arching into the air—four or five of them out of the water at the same time.

And then I recollected how, once before, many years back, I had seen such a school. Walking along the top of the dunes I had noticed a huge purple clot against the blue-green of the ocean. I was new to the Cape, those days, and bewildered by what I saw. I ran down the high dunes till I reached the edge of the water. And there I saw them: they turned the water to the color of wine. There were white bubbles and dimples all over the surface of the water, where the fish were jumping high to seize the feed. So close were they inshore that, had I not been fully dressed, I believe I could have waded out and seized them in my hands.

100

Young Roger had been feeling pretty low in his spirits. Summer after summer he had come here for his two weeks' vacation, and night after night he had stayed on the back shore with Tom, and never a strike had he had—no, not even a skate. (Tom had been getting so many skates this summer, that he had decided bitterly he should be subsidized to rid the Atlantic Ocean of these useless creatures.)

That particular evening the bass were quite a way out, so Roger went and got his boots on. I love to recollect the way he told the tale, and so I feel I must put it into his own words. They carry the conviction of a true experience.

"I must have cast about thirty feet," he said to an admiring audience, "just about thirty feet when he struck. He jumped out of the water and pounced on the plug and then ripped sixty-five yards of line off my reel and headed for the depths. I just started to reel in, and my drag was tight on his first run. He went first one side and then the other side, straight out to sea. And then, when he was tired out he started parallel with the shore, towards Provincetown, and I walked with him. It took me ten to fifteen minutes to get him in and beached. And it was a stiff job, for he started pulling me in because I had my drag so tight. He was hooked in the lower lip on one side, and that's what made him fight so hard."

The youngster paused, looking down with devotion upon the thirty-five-pound striper by his side.

"But he soon drowned," he went on. "He drowned because the water got into his mouth. And they don't last long like that."

On and on he talked, recounting every detail of the catch.

"My spool split from the strain of the line on it, and my left arm was dead from the effort. Luckily I had it beached, though, before the spool split. I tell you, I thought I had a whale on there."

101

I remember the feeling that had run through the entire beach, when they saw the size of the striper and knew of the fight he had put up. It was like a charge of electricity. There were stripers schooling all over the place, jumping right out of the water; but this was the only fish caught that night.

Dramatically, as the great fish had been carried up the beach by Roger and two of his friends, the hero of the evening collapsed upon the sand, breathless and pooped. The plug was still in his striper. He had not even the energy to unhook it. But neither would he let anyone else touch it. I watched him as he snarled to his buddy Tom.

"Stay away from it," he growled. "Can't you go and fish on your own?"

And the hero worship in the eyes of the younger boy turned to a visible hurt.

It is an intense world, this world of the striper, a world of atom plug and popping plug, plugs for splashing service and underwater plugs to imitate the crippled herring; jigs and rods and reels and spools. But never, with these ultra-perfectionists, anything in the way of bait. "Meatballers," they call them derisively—those who use squid or sand eels or the mere worm.

But, as I think of this, my mind switches to the other end of the social scale of fishing, and I find myself wondering if there is not perhaps more snobbishness about the sport of fishing than we like to admit.

For I am remembering a particular day when I went out with a family of three children and their father on one of those summer trips organized on Cape Cod.

Any authentic fisherman would have scoffed at us, for there we were with everything made easy: hand lines and bait, buckets and barrels for storing the fish we caught; even the knives and scrapers

102

for cleaning the fish on our return to port. No effort was demanded of us, and little skill. We merely stood with our hand lines against the rail of the boat, and waited. And, should we fail to catch a fish, there, attendant upon us, was the handsome young assistant to the captain—an electronics student from a Midwest university—to show us some of the tricks.

But it was a deeply enriching experience, and I doubt if any champion surf caster has enjoyed himself more.

I had additional delight that day because the children had taken this trip several times before; they were seasoned fishermen who could put me wise on everything, whereas I was a mere novice. I surrendered myself.

Standing there against the rail of the boat, I looked around me at our fellow fishermen. They were summer visitors and obviously people from the cities. This, today, was probably their one chance to touch upon the magic of fishing. What did it matter that the squid bait was handed to us, already cut into fitting portions, in little dixie cups, or that the only fish we were likely to catch would be the fairly worthless bony scup? The little *Sea Hawk*, pottering her way around in the waters of Nantucket Sound, held enchantment. Nothing, this day—this beautiful, clear day, with the northwest wind giving a clarity to the colors of sea and sky—nothing was beyond the realms of possibility.

"What did I tell you, Clare," whispered Cecily, the youngest child. "Didn't I tell you we were going deep-sea fishing? And here we are, beyond the harbor, right out at sea."

Actually we were only a few miles out when the *Sea Hawk* dropped her anchor and shut off her engines. Fortunately for the children's sense of wonder we were just beyond sight of land. This was no Georges Banks in a northeaster, but it held as much magic for us as if it had been the wildest and most desolate adventure.

The children—knowing better than anyone else, so they assured us—selected the best positions in the boat, where we would be certain to catch the most fish. And now Vincent handed me my reel.

"I'll fix your bait for you, Clare," he said with authority, selecting the fattest portions of squid for my hooks. "You see, I know

exactly how to do it. You must put it on double, or even triple, and try to hide the point of the hook so the fish won't see it. They're clever, you know. Nobody seems to realize how smart they are."

I nodded to my twelve-year-old mentor, rapidly assuming complete ignorance.

We dropped our lines over the stern of the boat—five thin strings with the leaden sinkers and the baited hooks—plumb to the bed of the ocean.

And then we waited, the lines twisted around the fingers of our right hands, so that we might be able to give the pull when we felt the tremor and shudder of the strike.

It was Kathleen who gave a squeal of delight as she drew in her line. There, dangling upon one of the baited hooks, wriggled a scup. We tossed it, slowly to die, to the bottom of our empty barrel.

We seemed to be having bad luck, for all around us the others were catching scups and rock bass and tautogs—beautiful brown-green creatures, with sepia markings and a delicate frillery of fin.

And then Vincent caught his first rock bass. This was followed by scups on the lines of both the girls. Only their father and I had still no luck.

Kathleen then had a mighty strike: on her line she found a sea robin and a blowfish.

I had no need to assume ignorance of the two fish, for I had never before seen them. Looking at them now, I found myself marvelling at the ingenuity of nature. Disentangling the sea robin from its hook, we saw this quirk in the balance of creation, this queer creature that seemed half-fish, half-bird, even to its croaking song. With the seemingly useless orange feet—so bird-like in color, like the feet of a fowl—and the dark, full wings, it was a strange merge between the world of the sea and the world of dry land.

But the children had turned their attention from the sea robin. They were looking sadly at the blowfish. After inflating himself, till he resembled an absurd, white, prickly balloon, he had become prosaically deflated, and, losing his magic, turned into an ordinary, utterly commonplace fish.

It was little Cecily who tried to comfort us.

"They say his tail is wonderfully good to eat," she told us, always resourcefully full of facts. "They say he's called a sea chicken, and that you can't even tell, when you eat the tail, whether you're eating chicken or fish."

But I was watching the boy. Something was going on in his head.

"I've got an idea," he said after a long silence. "I know Clare will want to draw this blowfish when we get it home, for she always wants to draw any fish we catch. I was watching it when it was inflated, and I think I know where it gets the air from. I'll bet you anything I can blow it up again, for Clare to draw. I've got it all thought out. I'll put my bicycle pump up against the hole there, just below the dorsal fin, and I'll make it look just as it looked now."

"It's a crazy world today," I told myself. "Wonderfully crazy —the sort of a world when anything could be made to happen."

Still we two grownups had caught nothing. The barrel was half filled with the fish the children had caught. We were surrendering to the next generation.

But each time I felt a nibble and jerked in my line, I failed to land a fish. Even the children grew worried.

It was nearing the moment when the *Sea Hawk*'s engines were due to start up for the return to port when our luck changed. Suddenly I began to haul in my fish. They were only scups, but numerically they could restore my pride. And then we got the boat's command: "Haul in your lines." At that precise moment, with the most accurate timing, the children's father caught his solitary scup. Everything in our world was perfect. The family honor was saved.

For the first time now, I was free to look down into the beauty of the water that rocked in the freshening northwest wind. It was deep green, warmed to a dull yellow in the sun. Upon its surface lay the exact shapes of our shadows as we leaned over the rail.

Returning to port, we cleaned our fish. Life had begun to ebb from them, and the eyes to glaze. The blowfish was dead and deflated, and the sea robin had renounced his sense of potential flight. Magic remained only in the eyes of the beholders.

The *Sea Hawk* docked. And little city men and their wives stepped ashore with the feeling that they had, this day, truly recaptured their rightful heritage.

We went back home, and the children's mother cooked the

106

bony little scups. I was forced to do my drawings, though, to tell you the truth, I was in no mood to work. Assisted and corrected by my young friend Vincent, I made an exceptionally bad drawing of a rock bass and a stiff, long-deceased sea robin. Finally I witnessed the fantastic drama of the reinflating of the blowfish. It was every bit as successful as the boy had promised.

Along he came with his bicycle pump. He had his two sisters in tow, provided with chewing gum and Scotch tape. When the poor dead fish had been blown up to the point where I feared it might explode and disgorge its insides upon us, Vincent promptly inserted his sister's warmed, chewed gum into the hole, just below the dorsal fin, and strapped it securely with Scotch tape.

"Now, Clare," he commanded me. "Draw like the very devil. For it won't stay like this very long."

That was a good day.

One day I went crabbing.

Crabbing is simple. Perhaps that is why I enjoy it. You merely get a ball of twine and attach a fish head to the end, with a pebble for a sinker. You toss this out into the middle of the creek, on the incoming tide, and wait.

I sought the beautiful blue crabs that are to be found only high up on the Cape. They abound in the salt-water creek at Osterville.

I think I felt sentimentally drawn towards them because of the past. I remembered a crab woman I knew in North Carolina, who lived alone in a pup tent under a sprawling live oak tree, near Manteo. Old Mrs. Reber went out early each morning around four o'clock, with her dip net and bucket, and crabbed all the day long in the sound. It was the season for soft-shell crabs and, even back in those distant years, they fetched a dollar and a half a dozen. I used to wade with her along the sound, and, when our buckets were filled, helped her dump the crabs into the square wooden buoy with a hole in it, where the crabs could stay alive in water. Around noon we would rest in the shade of the live oak, watchful always for rattlers and water moccasins and the deadly little coral snake. And she talked to me, scarcely seeing me, I felt, with those tiny eyes of hers all screwed up from looking for crabs so long, in the fierce southern sunlight. The tales she told me. . . .

But I am no longer in Albermarle Sound. I stand in water halfway up my thighs, in a tiny creek on Cape Cod. The tide rushes in, beneath the bridge. I feel the tug of a crab, and gently I pull the string towards me, until it is within easy reach of the net. Slowly, then—for crabs get easily net-shy—I push the net before me, across the sand bed of the creek, till the bait and the crab are within the confines of the net. I scoop my crab fully into the net and place it in the basket.

The blue crabs are lovely creatures: a dull olive-green on their top side, and a bony, ivory-white beneath, like the substance of the under part of the shell of a turtle. But it is the color of the lower side of the claws that is so particularly beautiful—a brilliant cerulean blue, tinged with ultramarine. And the tips of the claws are rosy crimson against the white teeth.

How often, feeling a little pull and a multiple nibble, I suppose I have caught my crab. But each time I draw in the string I find the fishhead bait surrounded by chub. These tiny scavengers of the creek seem to be here in the thousands. At the end of my string is no great blue crab weighing two pounds, as I have hoped. I look down through the water upon a pattern of swishing tails and quick-moving, miniature bodies, the color of the bed of the creek. They cover the bait with their marauding attacks, till the crabs can scarcely reach it.

It is late in the season and the crabs are beginning to feel the urge to bury themselves in the sandy mud of the creek banks until the warmth of next summer. In spite of this we bring back a basket full of the vicious, clawed creatures, crackling in their frightening imprisonment.

But we don't know what to do with them, and finally we give them away to the fisherman who had loaned us the nets.

As he handles one of the crabs it bites him and draws blood; but then I look, spellbound, watching him hypnotise the spiteful thing. He rubs it gently on its underside till suddenly it is so quiet that it appears dead.

It is October on the Cape, the season of the scallop. The flats are dotted, at low tide, with stooping figures. But these close-to-shore scallops they get are only the little ones. Here in the harbor of Wellfleet are the real draggers, scraping the bed of the bay. Inland from the shore, in little open sheds and outhouses, against groves of honey locusts, you will see the people opening the scallop. For here, since the early part of October, we think and live the scallop.

On the outskirts of Eastham, in an open shed, sit Captain Man'l and his wife. Over the long sunny hours of our Indian summer, throughout a Sunday afternoon they sit there, endlessly opening scallops. In half a month, he tells me, he has made three hundred dollars. Among the tall grasses of a clearing in the locust trees stands an enormous pile of empty scallop shells, the guts still sticking to them, smelling to the skies. He will sprinkle them with lime, and a road contractor from Rhode Island will come along and remove them and give him ten cents a bushel.

Meanwhile, they open scallops.

Onto the low wooden bench before them the heavy-jowled old man in the black sweater pours the scallops from the dank bushel sacks in the back of the shed. Nine of these sacks wait there, now

109

in midafternoon, where, earlier in the day, there had been fifteen.

"If she and me works well—" he tells me, heaving his great round body down upon the chair, "if we work hard we can open a bushel sack between us in thirty-five to forty minutes."

I watch them. Their hands seem a strange purple color. Their fingers are bound with rags to prevent the skin from wearing off.

"You can't be too careful about your hands," he says, noticing

that I am looking at these rags. "Have to keep your fingers from getting cut, you know, by the opening knife. Strange things, these scallop guts are. They're so poisonous that, if a cat was to eat them, its ears would fall off and they'd go right into the inside of the cat and it would most surely die. Poisonous things, they are, these guts. They'd infect the blood, I tell you. And it's so strong that if it lands on the paint of a boat it will stain it. Something very powerful about it."

I look at the guts as he opens the scallop shell and removes the "eye." And I remember watching scallops swimming in the bay. They swam backwards, propelling themselves by the action of opening and shutting, and, as they opened, the pockets inside were shiny black, like patent leather, and brilliant orange and rich peacock blue. But that was under the water, when they were alive.

Now, though, they hold a muted richness. The messy, shabby shells on the table, encrusted with little shiners like tiny blisters, are still beautiful, with their brown-golds and deep chestnut colors, and the dim slate grays.

"And did you drag them, Captain?" I ask him.

No, it seems, he doesn't have a boat these days. He has sold his, but aims to buy one next year, down to Wellfleet.

"But she won't let me," he adds, turning to his wife. "Says I'm too old."

The woman goes on opening scallops, scarcely pausing as she remarks: "I don't think much of people on boats on the water."

All these scallops everywhere, in the month of October; I feel I want to know more about how they are dragged. It isn't enough just to see them tossed upon a little wooden bench to be opened by Captain Man'l and his wife.

It's rough going, out in one of the A-frame, gibbet scallop draggers. The boat wiggle-waggles around as they drag under low power.

Barney laughs at me.

"You may think this is rough, but it's far worse when you're quahogging. And that's terrible for your boat, too. Have to use more power and keep your motor open all the while. And you're all on the side and you go round and round in circles and you dig deep down into the bed for the quahogs. That's when you toss and shake, I can tell you."

But the boat throws you around, even out scalloping, for it is the season, now, of winds and rough water. It is all right so long as the drag is out at the bottom; it acts then like an anchor and steadies the boat, slowing it as the drag fills up. But once that drag is lifted the boat surges suddenly ahead. We go out on the tide, to

111

get low water. The fishing is best then, the skipper tells me; the depth is less, and you can get quicker hauls and make better time.

"The high course tides don't fish as good," he adds, explaining scalloping to me as we stand together in the stern of the boat, by the culling board. "And drag fishing is better running with the tide. Doesn't have the tendency to lift and float as when it's against it."

And now a buoy is put down, and we drag in a wide circle, arching out from it, crisscrossing against it, scooping the bed of the bay.

Watching the two men in this dragger, the skipper manipulating the boat and his mate standing by the culling board to guide the bag as it swings, I realize that their world of knowledge is something very special. It is an unseen world. Whereas the surface of the water is all that concerns us, and all that we know anything about, these fishermen hold a mental picture of the bottom of the bay. To them it is like a printed page, whereon they can read where the "trash" is heaviest and know the varying types of sand. For they must be fairly sure of the great masses of marine growth and grass and ooze that could hit the bag and plug up the mesh so that it floats and the water can't get into it, and they are forced to take time to slat the bag clear and shake it.

"But sometimes you're fooled by this marine growth," says Barney. "You go and avoid that particular place, but along comes a high course tide and the current will remove it to somewhere else. It's a funny thing, and I've never been able to make it out, but marine growth works against the wind. A northeast wind will pull it up into the bay."

The first bag comes up. It swings in and lands on the stern of the boat, upon the culling board. It bulges like an enormous elongated sausage, a great big amber lantern, made of rust-colored iron mesh. Out from it pour the messy mysteries of the bay—moss and

112

shells and little rocks. The scallops are hidden among this "trash," as the fishermen call it.

But there are, also, crabs. Never have I seen more fierce-looking crabs at one moment. They come walking up to you from all directions. Carefully the men handle them in their thick gloves and throw them overboard. And then overboard goes all this wonderful "trash," the shoutingly bright, alarmingly colored sea-refuse, rich mahogany of weed, raucous green of sea lettuce, crimsons and browns and oranges beyond imagining. Back into the bay the men shovel them, with the rocks and the shells and the crabs, and the scallops are sorted and placed in the waiting buckets.

And now the puckering string is drawn up once more, and the bag swings out and is dropped into the water again.

The hours pass. The scallops stand harvested in the burlap sacks —three buckets to one sack—and the filled, dark sacks neatly balance the boat, ten on one side and ten on the other.

It is only when we have got our legal, daily quota of twenty bushels and are heading home for the harbor that Barney finds time to tell me yet more about scallop dragging. Listening to him and trying to learn all I can about his world, I begin to understand the preoccupation in the minds of fishermen as the scallop season grows near.

It is the never-ending obsession with the drag.

If you listen carefully you will hear snatches of conversation. Always, it seems, you will hear, like the chorus of a song, those words: "Then I had my drag out."

I like to remember the story of the fisherman's wife who went to choir rehearsal one evening and chanced to sit next to one of the most devout of men. He was deep in thought, and she knew well— for wasn't she, when all is said and done, a fisherman's wife?— that it was not of next Sunday's hymns that he was thinking.

She could stand it no longer. She leaned towards him and whispered in his ear: "I know, Henry. But do you think it will fish?"

And the man shook himself from his dreams and answered her: "But how ever did you happen to know I was worrying about my drag?"

It's a world of the drag, here on the Cape, in the fall and winter. Unlike the farmers of America, these fishermen have no county agents to advise them and report on developments and discoveries. They live on their own, and work on their own, and it is the result of their separate findings that will give them a good harvest or a skimpy one. Theirs is a never-ending battle. Always they are searching and thinking about the betterment of the drag. How do we improve the drag? is their constant question.

This same fisherman's wife told me of the first day her husband got his new drag.

"He beat that drag with his topping moll," she said. "And all the while he was beating it he was saying 'damn, damn, damn,' till I supposed his soul was well beyond saving. But, you see, he knew what he was doing. You've got to beat it with the moll to make it fish. It's just no good when it comes straight from the blacksmith's."

She paused, and I watched a whimsical smile cover her face as she added: "And then, after all that beating and swearing, sending your soul to hell, then you'll hit a rock and it's no good ever again."

And that was what Barney was really telling me, on our way back to the harbor.

"They're a temperamental thing, they are," he sighed. "We're always experimenting. It's not right yet, and you never know exactly why."

We near the wharf. The skipper is still talking about the drag.

114

"The tow line varies with the depth of the water," he is saying. "That's what makes the drag fish. And the scope is generally three times the depth of the water. You can tell if the drag is fishing by putting your hand on the tow line. And if the tow line is bouncing a little it means it's all right. But it must be a steady tremble, and if there's a longer interval between the bounce it means the drag is not fishing. And then the tow line has to be adjusted. . . ."

As I listen to him I begin to realize the total inadequacy of words. This fisherman may describe to me—and quite concisely and graphically—everything that happens to the tow line and the drag, but what really matters is that ultimate identification of the man with his tool. Working here with these two men in this boat, I may feel I know something about dragging. But it is the mere periphery. I cannot know the essence. That is to be learned after a lifetime of becoming one with the dragger and the bag, the tow line and the scallop. Yes, and one with the salt water itself, knowing its moods and its currents, the quality of its bed, and the way it surrenders to wind and moon, and the turn of the earth.

Coming back to the dock, my mind is filled with exact information about the size of the mesh of the bag; that this chain bag is good for only one season; that there is no way to find a drag after it's lost. All this is packed tight within my brain, as facts, yet I feel myself to be only little wiser. For I have learned even more deeply that a man's craft is something with which he has to live.

I look at these two fishermen, their faces tanned by the sun, but tanned in the strange inverted manner of fishermen, from below, from the sun reflected upon the sea, and protected from above by their visor caps. I look at them with their sense of quiet philosophy and patient servitude to the elements; and a humility enfolds me. But, because I am with these men, it is no belittling humility. It is a sudden feeling of expanse, and the power of growth.

The Wellfleet Oysterhouses

It is a noble clump of buildings. The gray shingles have been silvered so long by the salt air that they have a burnished glow, like the breast of a dove. But, beautiful though these oysterhouses may be, with their honest structure and the perfection of their setting, they yet carry a poignancy. Looking at them, you feel you confront the dead past. They hold the sadness of all buildings that are no longer in use.

It is not exactly right to say that they are no longer in use. To some extent they have redeemed themselves in their old age and are dying gracefully; they have become the Mecca of the artist.

This is not surprising, for it is a fantastically picturesque group, changing in mood with each shift in the light and every variation

117

in the weather. Come here on a typical summer day, when a northwest wind brings clarity to the land, and they gleam in this light. Duck Creek, around them, is unbelievably blue. The grasses fringing the feet of the houses shout in their brilliant green. (It is the green of my childhood, I remember suddenly, the particularly raucous color in my cheap paint box, called green bice.) On such a day the shadows are sharp-edged and simple. This is not the mood of subtlety.

But come to them on a silvery, misty day, one of those days that hold the greatest beauty here on Cape Cod. Fog films the sun, and everything is muted. In this light the oysterhouses are charged with mystery. It is a lost world, a world of seeking, finding, and again losing the shapes before you.

The summer artists who surround these oysterhouses with campstools and easels rarely know the visual drama of the buildings under the light of winter. I happened to live across the creek from them one year, and watched their obedience to each mood of the sky. Gulls spotted the silhouettes as winter approached, screaming and circling above the roofs. The movement of the birds gave a queer, frail sense of instability to these stocky buildings, and seemed to emphasize the disintegration that was setting in, under the stress of Cape storms, over the years.

And then there would be the winter sunsets, violent and wild. I remember one special evening: The earth was cold and the wind blew through one's skin, into the bones. All the day long the sky had been gray. A gloomy day, you could truthfully have called it, a day to obliterate. But, with the setting of the sun, a complete orchestration of color flashed upon the scene, in scarlet and crimson, against the sullen gray. At this little moment, lasting at most ten minutes, the landscape became unbelievable in its crazy beauty. The sun went down in apocalyptic glory. It was the world of the

Book of Revelations. Duck Creek was the color of lead, like thunderclouds that had fallen into the water. The upper sky had remained leaden gray. At this time of year the raucous green grasses had turned to buff; they shone now like gold. Upon the water lay little white boats. Suddenly every boat turned deep pink against this sea of ink.

Pulled backwards in time, as one so often is at moments of sudden excitement and emotion, I found myself repeating the words of an English nursery rhyme:

> If all the world were apple pie,
> And all the sea were ink,
> And all the trees . . .

But nothing further mattered in this childhood jingle. For here, before my eyes, I saw at last that "all the sea was ink."

This blaze of scarlet and crimson lit fires in the broken glass of all the windowpanes of the oysterhouses, till they glowed as though it were for a celebration. Once again, for a little space of time, the houses appeared inhabited.

It was at this particular moment that I seemed to realize the life that had been lived within these buildings, a life when the windowpanes must always have glowed like this.

I was listening to the stories of the past, told me by Silas King.

"Nobody knows what those oysterhouses really mean to us," he said. "They aren't just buildings, standing there for the artists to paint—though these summer artists seem to think the town ought to maintain them just as they are, so as they can go on painting them. We stay away these days, those of us who knew something of what they meant, for it doesn't seem right they should be treated as they are today—just something to make a picture of. . . . They were the center of our life, way back over the years."

Silas King sat deep in his chair this rainy evening in late December. The wind howled around his house. The heat from the coal stove felt good.

"They were a busy place," he went on. "Those were the days when Wellfleet oysters were something to be proud of—not that they aren't still, so big and good they are. The circular cellars in these old Cape Cod houses weren't built for hurricane shelters, as most people seem to think; they were where we used to store our oysters during the winter, and still do. We always put oysters away in our cellars in November and December, either to eat or sell—nine to ten bushels, at the very least—to have them accessible when the weather got frozen. We'd keep them in barrels lined with paper against the frost, standing them well away from the walls so the air could circulate around them. Oysters are best when they're feeding upon themselves. They 'open' better—meaning, I might say, that there's more quantity to the oyster—when they have been kept out of the water for a while."

Listening to this man, I began to see, unfolding before me, the saga of the Wellfleet oyster.

"We used to send our oysters to England and Europe, back in 1906," he went on. "Sent them—from these houses out behind here—as a gift to King Edward the Seventh, of England. Sent them, I've been told, to the German Kaiser, too, so as not to make him jealous. They went across the ocean in barrels, each separate oyster wired to prevent it's opening up and losing its liquid. We wired them to stop them from opening up their mouths and laughing, we always used to say. They can stay alive fully three months, so long as their liquid remains inside them, and they don't get dry. We packed them carefully in barrels, so the bills weren't injured. Placed them deep side down. The liquid stays in, that way."

Silas seemed a fitting descendant of Thoreau's Oysterman.

"I remember those days," he said. "There were beds all up the bay to Brewster Channel. The west side of the bay was reserved for quahogs."

"But what about the oysterhouses?" I interrupted him. "What used to happen there?"

"Oh," he answered me slowly, as though he were thinking back with difficulty to those remote years. "That's where we used to cull out the oysters. There were five culls: box oysters (those were the very biggest, and whopper creatures they were, to be sure); then came large; next medium; then medium small; and last of all, small. Never could get them mixed up, I can tell you. Always had to keep them apart. We worked there all the day long during the oyster season, with barrel packing and shipping into the freight cars. You know those railroad tracks that are all rusty now?"

He broke off, pointing out of the dark window to where the tracks still lay.

"They never got a chance to get rusty in those days. Always busy with the trains that would pick up the barrels of oysters and take them to Boston. The sidings ran right along by the oyster-houses, and all you had to do was to move the barrels over into the freight cars. And then, when you were waiting for more oysters to come in, or when the train might be a bit late, you enjoyed your-selves. None of the smutty talk and the deep drinking you get at some places. People like to suppose we lived a hell of a life there; but we didn't. We were working too hard. It was just cribbage and poker. . . . There'd always be some old-timers in the back part by the stove, playing two-handed games and soaking up the heat. And then, while we were waiting, there'd be four-handed games all over the place. It was kind of warm and good for the old-timers, spending their entire days there. Reminded them of the work they used to do. But we never let them worry us."

121

The look of reminiscence had clouded Silas King's eyes. And then a sudden twinkle came into them.

"Do you know what," he said. "I was suddenly thinking. Those oysters go a long way back. The Indians ate them, of course, and had to keep on moving to new camps when the piles of shells got too big and too smelly. Filthy creatures, they must have been. . . . But then there was a chap called Lopez—a Portuguese— and they say he transferred oysters to Salem back in 1650. And the Pilgrims, a few years later, shipped pickled oysters to England in barrels, all dried and smoked. They used to string them to cure them. Now what I've been thinking is, how come we are such fools today? Why don't we start in and pickle and smoke and dry them? Nothing much better to eat, that I can see, than a pickled oyster."

We sat silent, then, for a long while. He was busy dreaming up a dramatic revival for his oyster.

But he still had much to talk about, from the past.

"In the cold weather it was a tough job, culling out those oysters. We used to wear woolen mittens. They were hand-knitted, and strong. They kept on shrinking as they got wet, and this thickened them and made them warmer. Not that our hands weren't tough anyhow, though we did wear a rubber 'cot' on our fingers, to protect them when we culled. Tough? Why, our hands were hard as rawhide. I remember Nat Delory; he could light a match in the palm of his hand. It wasn't any showing off, either. He did it as a matter of course, it was so natural to him. They were rugged, those days, I can tell you. . . . Nat went quahogging till he was eighty. All he knew was hard work. And he'd raised about twenty-five children. I remember how he upped and married a widow with ten children, when he was getting on in life. Fed them all right, too, so that they grew up to be good workers."

122

Listening to these tales of earlier days, when life here in Wellfleet had hummed with work, I thought of the derelict oysterhouses, falling away, one after the other, and leaving great gaps, like teeth coming from an old man's mouth. These tokens of a bygone age were worthy of respect. One of them, I knew, had been floated across the creek to be used as a work shed. Two others, just recently, had been bought by a sentimentalist in Wellfleet, to save them from tumbling into the water. With great difficulty and much affection he had removed them, intact, to his own place inland in the woods. And there they now stand, as safe as though they were in an old people's home. But, despite the worthy intentions of this man, something is wrong. These oysterhouses belong here, in Duck Creek, their feet in the water even at low tide, and their thighs hidden beneath this water when the tide has turned and the sea rushes up the creek and under the railroad tracks, till it submerges the clumps of grass around Uncle Tim's Bridge.

But Silas's voice crept into my thoughts. He was still talking.

"They were never idle," I heard him say. "Once October came they were used for scallops. The women were there, too, opening the scallops. . . . And then came the oysters in the winter. And of course we had the quahogs in the summer. No, we were never idle. . . . But somehow or other, though there were always so many of them around in Wellfleet, we never seemed to have many of the Finns there. They kept pretty much to themselves. Came for the quahogging, at the beginning, and then began to move away when the quahogging got bad. A rugged, powerful people they were. And their women were powerful massive creatures, too, and would work alongside the men. They used to haul their men home when they'd had a bit too much to drink. . . . It's a funny thing, but drink hits the Finn quick. He can't hold out against it. . . . The women used to haul their men home across the ice and through the freezing water, cloppety, cloppety, clop, over the rough boards of Uncle Tim's Bridge, towing them behind them over the frozen ground. The tales I've heard, and the things I've seen. . . ."

He murmured on. Fantasy was taking over.

The next time I visited the oysterhouses I felt respect and tenderness that was stronger even than before. I understood now a little more of their past. Proudly they stand there, bulwarked by shells. This, beneath them, is neither sand nor mud. Go down there at low tide, and you will see that the structure of their foundations is composed of scallop, quahog, sea clam and oyster shells. Mummified shells lie there, lathed by the muddy tides over so many years that they have lost all individual coloring and retain mere brittle, fluted forms.

Your feet crunch upon them, and destroy them, but always there are layers upon layers of new shells to take their place. It is as though we tread on the stacked ware of a china factory, so orderly are they. They stand there, in a fascinating, complicated pattern of sharp-edged, up-ended swirls. How did it happen that they are so neat? Could they possibly have been arranged like this? It is like the ordered design in nature: the hexagonal forms of a honeycomb, the center of a daisy, the stamens of a flower. Are they the result of the endless lapping of water, in the rushing tide, stroking the shell piles that have been tossed here from the shucked scallops and sea clams, and the culled oysters?

And then I remember the men in their boats coming up into Duck Creek in the early spring. With that fling of the body which is instinctive in the spring of the year, the same fling that has sown seed upon the earth since the beginning of time, the fishermen shovel the shells they have made during the fall and winter. That same twist from the waist, that identical circular toss from the extended arms, sows shells upon the watery earth, as a home for the oyster spat. This may be water, rather than a cornfield, but it holds the same needs and requires the same germinal gestures. Among these empty, discarded shells, upon them and within their innermost interstices, the baby oysters will make their nursery, needing always the mother shell upon which to stand and grow.

Not all the shells here have lost their color. Beneath the water, at the far edge beyond the furthermost building, they glow in pinks and greens, stained deeper by the water. But even those shells, though wet, lack the richness of color of the whorled ranks under the shelter of the oysterhouses themselves, where they are protected from the bleaching force of the sun. These are more perfect of shape, fluted and subtle, dense coral-pink and sage-green, orange and mauve.

It is a late afternoon in the fall. Duck Creek is so calm that the dilapidated gray buildings are precisely doubled in the water. I hear a clattery noise, carried clearly across the creek. A fisherman has come out from behind the houses with a barrow. He is spilling scallop shells upon the ground, adding to this pile that is becoming the earth itself.

It is a comforting sound, this clattery noise, for it gives dignity to the oysterhouses. They are dying with integrity.

Shipwreck

A freighter had come aground. She had washed at Peaked Hill Bars, outside of Provincetown.

It was really the result of the threatened hurricane, which, although it was veering out to sea, yet had badly disturbed our weather. Overnight the Cape had been shrouded in sudden dense fog—one of the worst fogs in many years, they later said.

This little Greek freighter was manned by a crew who could not speak English. Only the ship's cook knew a few words, and he was busy in the galley preparing the meals. And so none of them were much aware of the state of the weather, for they could not understand the reports that came over the radio. But they got scared of the fog, as all seamen do.

To their starboard they saw a light. Actually it was the flash of the Highland Light, piercing the fog into the Atlantic. But the Greeks mistook it for the light of Race Point. They knew this meant shelter and steered towards what they supposed was Race Point to get around Long Point into the harbor of Provincetown.

127

And so the freighter fetched up on the treacherous sand bars of Peaked Hill, adding one more vessel to the roster of wrecks that had earned for these shoals the name of The Graveyard of the Atlantic.

I was camping on the sand dunes across from Provincetown, this night of fog and storm. We were in a shack, set into a dip of the dunes, within sight of the ocean just opposite to the Peaked Hill Bars. We had stayed up late, talking, for we felt tense and somewhat apprehensive as to what the storm might bring. Outside the shack we faced opaque fog. We were lost in a world of fog.

Around one or two in the morning we decided to bunk down. Our histrionic sense of courage had begun to ebb. Each one of us felt the first undeclared symptoms of the need for individual self-protection. The mood of drama was fast fading.

It must have been about four o'clock when I heard someone stirring. I turned in my bunk, and listened. But I was so deeply sleepy that only vaguely was I conscious of a voice saying:

"There are lights out there. I think the fog must have lifted. But I don't know what the lights mean, or what they are. Do you suppose it's a beach buggy on a crazy midnight cruise? Or could it be some surf casters staying out late, waiting for stripers?"

I must have gone back to sleep. I knew nothing until early morning.

The fog had disappeared, to be followed by a fury of wind and rain. Into the sound of the wind was woven the hammering thump of the breakers.

Dazed still from our few hours of sleep, we stumbled across the dunes to look at the ocean. This storm, we knew, would give dramatic beauty that we must not miss.

But we were not prepared for what actually we saw.

Before us, like a picture painted by a surrealist artist, lay a

128

stranded vessel. It seemed fantastically enormous, there at the fringe of the shore. The rain fell out of the skies in sheets, solid water coming down upon us as it must have done in the days of Noah in his ark. It was drenching us, but we were beyond awareness of ourselves. Suddenly, without warning, we were caught up into tragedy.

For we realized we faced an authentic disaster and that we were no longer mere spectators. We had been forced into the role of protagonists. We must try to save this ship, stranded upon the sand bars.

Something, we decided, must have gone wrong with her radio. The men from the Coast Guard station, else, would already have been here. In an instant flash of realization, the way one can react always in a crisis, we knew what to do. One of us got into the jeep and rushed to Race Point, to check with the Coast Guard and see if they were alerted. This was no stage setting of a shipwreck. Human lives were waiting to be saved.

To those of us who stayed behind on the beach, it seemed an endless time before the coastguardmen arrived. Out there beyond reach, in the curdling water, tossed by this violent wind, lay the freighter. The waves were so high that they almost covered the ship.

Soon, though, through the blinding rain, we saw we had been perceived. The ship tried to heave a line to us on the shore; but, though the wind was actually with them, they yet couldn't get the line over on this wind, which seemed to swirl in circles around the vessel. Time after time the line wavered in the air, tossed and twisted by the wind, till it fell limp into the boiling sea. A surge of impotence swept over us, as we stood there at the edge of the raging water. There was no possibility of swimming out to the line. The waves were thirty feet high. No one could brave that sea.

It was a desperate feeling, standing there safely on the sand, unable to help. The freighter rode high, as though she were in ballast. And yet, knowing this particular part of the shore, we were aware that she must be stuck fully four to five feet deep into the sand bars. There was absolutely nothing we could do, but wait for the coastguardmen from Race Point.

And then they came. They shot a cannon with the line and secured the breeches buoy.

Twelve of the Greeks came to shore on this breeches buoy. And as they landed on the beach, stunned and tense from the strain, we noticed for the first time that the freighter's lifeboat had been tossed upon the sand.

We were about to walk towards this lifeboat, wondering why the crew had not used it as a means of coming ashore, when we saw that the big line had broken and the thirteenth man had been dropped into the swirling cauldron of the sea.

I had never before seen a man in danger of death. We shouted to him, telling him to hang on to the breeches buoy; but the Greek could not understand what we were saying. Three great waves washed over him, and it looked for a few moments as if he were doomed. But the tide was in his favor, and finally he was washed towards the shore.

Forgetting the force of the sea we waded out into the raging waves and managed to drag him up to the dry sand. He was a pitiful sight, limp and unconscious from exhaustion. I looked down upon him as he lay there, and a sense of compassion overcame me. He was an elderly man, with none of the resilience of youth. We carried him over the sand and up the dunes to the shelter of our shack. But he remained unconscious. And then the coastguardmen took him away with the other Greeks, and we were relieved that no longer did we need to concern ourselves about him.

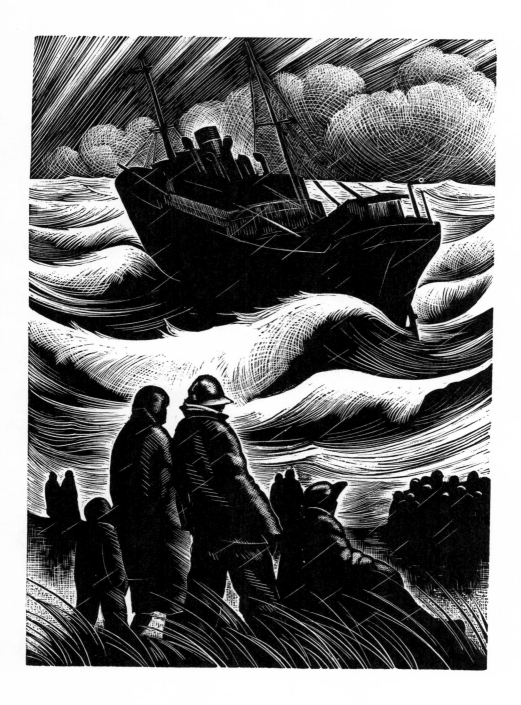

But it wasn't so easy, I found, to get him out of my mind. I kept on seeing this cold, gray-skinned face and the heavy, limp body, and I yearned over him, wanting to help cherish him back to life.

It was midmorning by now, and the rain had ceased, giving way to an oppressive, sticky heat. Every effort seemed exhausting. The scene began to change as rumors of the wreck spread. The crowds started to trickle across the dunes like thin lines of black ants. Sightseers gravitated towards the beach, drawn by the magnet of this wreck.

For a shipwreck appeals to the sense of human drama. Here, before them, direct and at first hand, in a world given over to substitute living, was the actual plot of a movie. There was no need now to go to see it on the screen. Even the expressions held magic: "shipwreck"; "lifeboat"; "breeches buoy"; "survivors." These brought back the days of childhood and the adventure stories we had read. Not often did they come our way in real life.

It so happened that this shipwreck took place in the early hours of Labor Day. This was fortunate, for it meant that the entire population of Provincetown, as well as the people up the Cape—the news having spread far and wide—were free to visit the scene of the disaster. Beach buggies made a fortune, plying between Provincetown and the outer shore. Press photographers and newspaper reporters were on the spot. It was a dramatic finish to the season of summer vacationists, an unexpected bonus. Over the three miles of sand they trickled, the sturdy ones ignoring the help from the constant beach buggies, plodding across the sand in the sticky heat. Before them, urging them forward as their spirits flagged, stood the masts of the freighter and the top of her smokestack, strangely discordant in this setting, standing high above the ridge of the next sand dune, standing always, when that ridge had been exhaustingly crossed, above the ridge of a further dune, till

133

it seemed as though one could never reach the actual shore. People who would never have supposed they could walk so far trudged this day in the heat across the desert of sand behind Provincetown, lured by the promise of a wreck. Women carried small children in their arms. Elderly people dragged their faltering footsteps across this torrid expanse of sand—sand that was loose beneath the feet, dominating sand that sucked them down into its depths.

But something more than the spectacle of a shipwreck drew the Cape Codders. Unbeknownst, they were acting in obedience to a memory.

For it was in the great tradition. Shipwrecks were in the blood of their forebears, way back, across the centuries. Something of this race memory smolders within them still. The word "shipwreck" brings release to them from the twisted, subdued routine of today, when the Cape is being given over to caring for vacationists. During the months of summer, as cars from the forty-eight states of America invade their territory, the Cape Codders never feel entirely happy. Deep below their conscious awareness they have a sense of shame, as though they are betraying their heritage.

At the peak of their pride and their power, these Cape people were America's whalers and fishermen. They built ships, and went to sea, living fully and dangerously. For weeks and months at a time the men stayed far out in the Atlantic, braving northeasters and the winter gales.

This spirit within them still lives. Fraily undernourished, it awaits some incident from the outside to make it flame into a rich fire of action. At the mere mention of a shipwreck, all the latent passion of the seaman comes to the surface. The demoralizing clutter of the summer season is rejected.

They flocked to the scene, feeling suddenly at home.

There were still many men aboard the freighter. We could see

134

them, looking like tiny, frightened insects. At any moment the vessel could heel over into the sea, for her rudder had split and her propeller shaft had broken, and she had had engine trouble and was out of control.

Only now, in a pause of the drama, did I become fully aware of the lifeboat, derelict upon the beach, high above the tide lines. It was surrounded by a condemning crowd of old-timers.

It was a useless thing, rotted away from the underneath part of the gunwale. You could reach inside and flake off scraps and layers of loose iron. Holes showed all over it, and it was splotched with rust. Looking at the lifeboat, I felt no surprise that the crew had not dared to come ashore in it. They had tried to launch it, but it was so rotten that when two seas hit the boat it broke in pieces. The hawser parted and the big seas crushed it against the side of the freighter. It just crumbled—like egg shell, as seamen always say—and broke in its sides.

Two of the severest critics of this stranded life boat were retired members of the Life Saving Service.

"When you think of the surf boats we've known," one of them boasted. "Remember the Race Point model that Charlie Gardner designed—the best ever? It was rowed single bank and had a narrow stern to prevent broaching to, and a bluff bow to give buoyancy in getting off the beach."

"Yes," added the second old man. "And its oars were fourteen feet long."

Seeing me standing next to them, they realized they had found an audience. One of them turned to me.

"Those fellows in the Life Saving Service were boatmen, I can tell you. Like to know how we launched a surf boat?"

There was nothing I would enjoy more, and I assured them so.

"They don't do it so much these days, you see. They've got

those queer things they call ducks," he explained. "You had to know how to row. You had to launch that boat, even if it got smashed on the beach. And you had to know your surf. There are always three waves, it seems. And then comes a lull. And you've got to be keen about this, and then, just after the third wave, in this lull, you get out and cover the distance before the next sea cobbles up. I was bow oarsman, because I was lighter than the others. I was the first man out, when we got back."

"Yes," interrupted the other man. "And there were five men and the captain, and there was plenty of room—a full five-foot leverage. We had to watch the stroke oarsman so that we could all row in with him. In a surf boat like that you never feathered your oars. It wouldn't do. You'd catch the wind. . . . And when we got near to the beach—for it was always near the beach you got your real seas—the captain'd shout 'Boat oars,' or more likely just 'Oars,' and you'd come in speedily, just like one of those airplanes. But it's tricky, I can tell you. Got to know your surf."

"And that was why we had to have such drill, always," added his companion.

More and more people had joined the crowds on the beach. Not for a long while had I seen so many old-timers at this season of the year. They seem to disappear, always, during the summer, and can be observed only during the fall and winter. But the shipwreck had brought them out. They stood in groups, waiting for something to happen. And as everyone waited they talked, till the lull became a social gathering.

All around me I could overhear sentences beginning with "I remember," or "Do you remember?"

The shipwreck was forcing them backwards in time.

I wandered among them, greedy for the richness of their past.

". . . the terrible things that happened. Once, when they were

136

rescuing men from a wreck, the boat's main boom swung around and hit the surf boat and stove it in and sunk it. . . . The lighthouse keeper was one of the crew with five others and he was drowned. . . . The son came on, in another surf boat, and picked up the body and found it was his father. . . . But he went on and saved the others and got to the wreck. Every winter there were some men drowned in those surf boats. Every winter . . ."

"Wooden vessels didn't ever break up like a tanker. And a steamer is the weakest thing. They break in two. They've no give or twist. They can't take it. It was nothing for a fisherman to be up on the beach for two or three days when he had a wooden ship. But nowadays these metal things just snap in two."

Listening to these men I found myself remembering the motto of the old Life Saving Service: "You've got to go out, but nobody says you've got to get back."

And then, just as I was thinking about this, I met up with an old pal of mine from Wellfleet. He, too, was a retired Life Saving Service man.

"All this makes you think," he said, nodding his head out to the stranded freighter. "Makes you think back, it does. I remember the day the Italian bark *Castagna* came ashore. Ma'd sent me down early to the store, that morning, to get some coffee or flour—I forget which. I was around twelve years old, then, and still going to school, and hadn't ever missed a day. But when I was in the store, getting these things for Ma, I heard the men telling of a vessel that had come ashore, over by the Marconi wireless. So just like that I played hookey. The only time in my life, too. I tore back home to Ma, without saying a word, making it look like I was in a hurry to get to school. But instead I walked over to the back shore. . . . Just as I was getting near the back shore, who do I see but Joe Curran with his wagon. It was a bright blue wagon, I remember well.

137

" 'Hi, there,' he called me. 'Look what I have in back.'

"So I climbed up the wheels, and looked inside. I never was more surprised in my life. Four naked bodies lay there in Joe Curran's wagon, frozen stiff, they were, and their eyes were wide open and stared straight at me. And there, down the front of the leg of one of the fellows, was the perfect imprint of an axe, where they'd had to hack him off from the rigging.

" 'Got any more?' I asked.

" 'You'd better get along down there to the back shore and you'll see,' shouted Joe, as he whipped up his horse and went on to town."

My Wellfleet friend was just about to continue with the story of this wreck when one of his buddies came along and interrupted.

"It makes you feel all queer, doesn't it," he said, "looking at a wreck again, after all these years? It makes you begin to think about boats. Boats are strange things. There's something about a boat that has a spirit—just like you and me. And when they disappear it's as if they die and their spirit dies, too."

We were joined then by yet another old-timer. The stranded freighter was drawing them all closely together.

"Yes," murmured the newly arrived seaman. "These wrecks make you do a bit of thinking. Looking at the vessel there, on the Peaked Hill Bars, where there must be so many lying down at the bottom of the ocean, reminds me of when I had my dragger. You take a trip to Georges Banks and you're sailing over graves—the bed of the ocean is packed and crowded with them, the same as here. Nobody will ever know how many there are. There've been wrecks just there over centuries. And then you begin to wonder what you'll bring up. You get a funny feeling that you're disturbing the bones of your ancestors—your own family. There are fellows you've known down there, too. For all you can tell you

138

might be dragging them up in the dragger, in with the sea clams and the fish. You bring up all kinds of things in that dragger: worn-out pieces of wreckage, and all, and it might just as likely be some of your great grandfather's own bones. I tell you, as you sit there in your boat, with the engine throbbing and throbbing, on and on, you begin to think about things and you begin to wonder. You begin to wonder if they're with you, out there. And then you can almost feel them around you. . . . And you wonder what they were thinking and feeling at the last, when they went down. . . ."

"God, they've been a lot of wrecks," added my Wellfleet friend with sad finality.

Enticed by these Cape memories, I began to think, then, of the shipwrecks on the Outer Banks of North Carolina. That was a world formed by the wrecks of the past, bringing to its culture people from alien civilizations, men from Devon, speaking still, today, with their West of England tongue, men from Persia, men who, as the bankers call the shipwrecked sailors, "have come ashore as a grown man."

We were, each one of us, sinking deeper and deeper into the past.

It must have been around five o'clock that a stir came into the waiting crowd. And, because all this was taking place in that no man's land between high-water mark and low, one sensed a strange, indefinable, yet evident tension in the atmosphere. At first I wondered what it was, but as, more and more, the people started to question the nature of the freighter's cargo, I began to understand what was happening.

The age-old instinct of the wrecker had lifted its head. This urge, stretching backwards in time—the same urge that gave birth to the mooncussers, with their habit of carrying lights along the shore to inveigle ships into supposing they were heading for harbor, this same impulse that gave its name to Nags Head, in North Carolina, where the natives, in the far distant past, used to tie a lantern to the head of a nag and let her loose to roam the beach as a decoy to ships at sea—this, now, with the Greek freighter stranded there a mere hundred yards offshore, was asserting itself, beyond all conscious awareness or control. As the hours passed, more and more people asked questions about her cargo. Already the derelict lifeboat had been stripped of all available loose parts, to be taken home as trophies.

But her cargo? What of that? Fantastic rumors began to float around. We had ascertained that she was from Nova Scotia and bound for Baltimore. We had discovered, too, that she was in ballast. But the fact that she had a Greek crew gave rise to the wildest speculations. One Portuguese woman, in all seriousness, informed me that her cargo had been monkeys and peanuts.

"I know it, for sure," she assured me. "My brother is the boatswain's mate of the duck that is on its way here, and he told me. The only trouble is that they let the monkeys go overboard and then felt they ought to send the peanuts after them for the monkeys to feed upon."

A sense of frustration welled up in the crowd. The freighter was in ballast. There would be nothing to pillage. The race memory of these Cape Codders was in revolt. Not that they were ever really mooncussers, in the strictest sense of the word, like the men of Block Island. Nobody could ever say that of them. But, after all, what was a shipwreck for if you couldn't get something out of it?

Recollections of past wrecks came to the surface, tales told by fathers and grandfathers of lumber and liquor, fish and flour, cashew nuts and even marshmallows that had been washed ashore.

140

"We lived for months on blueberries and frozen salmon," said a fisherman's wife. "A disappointing cargo it was, believe me. Never want to eat salmon again in my living days."

"I remember the time when a ship was wrecked off Handkerchief Shoal, way up-Cape, near Chatham and Orleans," said an old man. "There was enough liquor to last us the whole winter through, even though they were heavy drinkers, those days, too. And the quarterboards they used to get—great, mighty carved and painted things they were, fine to put up over your barn. . . . Those were the days of real wrecks, I tell you."

"And there's many a part of the *Portland* is supporting a store or a porch in Wellfleet," added another. "And I happen to know for a truth that the cover of the hole of my own privy came from a piece of the case of some dynamite from the *Longfellow*."

"And I shall never forget the tales of the night when the *White Squall* came ashore. My aunt was there, I remember. Her cargo was dragon's blood and spices—all the way from Calcutta, India, it was."

The Greek freighter was betraying them. It was an anticlimax.

All the same, every able-bodied grown man and every small boy in that crowd of watchers intended, before the freighter had been hauled off the shoals, to make a try at landing on the vessel.

"I'd like just to see if it's true that she's carrying nothing," said an old Portuguese fisherman. "Never feel you can quite trust a foreigner's word about anything. No, I say. Never can trust a foreigner."

Out there, on the deck of the freighter, stood the rest of the crew, waiting. The sea raged, with little sign of any quietening. The breeches buoy line, still strung between the vessel and the top of the sand dunes, tautened and slacked rhythmically, as the freighter rocked in the force of the waves. The anchor line hung loosely down into the waves, no longer of use in the raging sea.

"What are we all waiting for?" the crowds began to question. "What is going to happen now?"

They were beginning to feel that the scene before them lacked drama. They clumped in little family groups among the beach grasses. Hours were passing, and nothing was taking place.

"Why don't they do something?" asked one old woman. She was exhausted still from her pilgrimage across the dunes. She wiped her brow and sighed with fatigue. "Come to think of it, I scarcely know why I let you haul me all across these miles. Could have been resting, seeing as it's Labor Day and all."

But her old man beside her was lost in thought.

"Just you keep quiet, Lizzy," he scolded her. "Don't you see there's still living souls out there on that freighter? Got to let them know we're watching for them and waiting. Got to, I tell you."

Suddenly there was a stir and ripple in the crowd. Someone with strong field glasses had seen it out in the distance along the sand.

"The duck's coming!" the cry went up. "The duck's over there, from Nauset."

The wreck had flung me backwards in time. So much so that I had been confused, somewhere inside me, because this was not a sailing ship that had fetched up on the bars. The word "shipwreck" seemed to belong to the past, before the days of radio and and radar. I kept on thinking of clipper ships and schooners, all of them with tattered sails, and was finding it difficult to bring the event up to the present day. And so it was that it took me some little while to grasp what was meant by the "duck."

But then I saw it. The amphibian arrived, manned by the Nauset men. The ripple of excitement had grown into a great wave. As they reached the shore just in front of the stranded freighter, a loud cheer rose from the waiting crowd. Drama had returned.

I looked then at the crew who manned this amphibian. Here were the rightful descendants of the old Cape Codders. I saw no deviation from type. They were lean-faced men with a background of sea and storm, fearless and prepared for danger.

Tension gripped the beach, as the duck took off into the angry sea. It made a wide detour, aiming to reach the freighter alongsides. Violently it tossed in this rough sea, till you began to fear lest it might not be able to make it. Three times it tried to come alongside, and three times it failed. Up there, on the deck of the Greek freighter, stood a row of tiny black figures, waiting against the rope ladder. Finally we saw the amphibian just beneath the ladder, and the tension in the crowd upon the beach became almost visible as we watched while, one after the other, these tiny black specks crawled down the ladder, like scared ants, to be caught into the duck.

The white, angry waves lapped the duck and tossed her against the side of the freighter till we felt sure she would be crushed to pieces.

When the duck returned to shore, we saw that there remained a half dozen or so men still on the deck of the ship.

Silence covered the waiting crowds as the Greek survivors emerged from the amphibian. They were a dark, grim, unsmiling set of men, bewildered and stunned still by what they had gone through. At the exact moment when they stepped upon the sand, the tension broke. An enormous cheer went up from the people around. This cheer enfolded the strange, unsmiling Greeks, and their rescuers, till the entire beach became a riot of rejoicing and applause.

But there, sitting by himself on the amphibian, was the navigator. As I looked more closely at him, with his strong face, I saw that he trembled. It was not the trembling of a weak man.

143

"I didn't like it," he said to me. "I just didn't like it, I tell you. It was only by the grace of God we got them off safely. Never known a wilder sea. Thought we'd be crushed against the freighter, at any minute, like egg shell. Had to keep her just the slightest distance from the boat, so as we wouldn't be beaten against it. Thought we were done for, several times."

His strain made him ashamed, and automatically, in self-defence, it turned into a resentment.

"And then, after all that, they go and stay there," he spat. "The captain and six of the crew just won't come off when we tell them to. Can't understand a word of what we say to them, either, even when we shout. And there we are, liable to be battered to bits against their ship, yelling to them to come down the rope ladder, and all they do is to shake their heads. What they don't seem to know is that we are responsible for them. Suppose I'll have to stay out here all the night long, just watching to see the ship doesn't heel over, owing to her hull damage, and they get drowned."

And yet, I felt like reminding him, deep down inside you, in your real self, you know very well that in their place you would have stayed on your ship—and not only because of the mere detail of ship lore, of salvage of a deserted ship. It would have been something way back in your past, long before you were conceived, that has given you the strong, good look in your face.

But the navigator went on trembling throughout his body.

I left him. Out there the Greek freighter stood high in the water, her rudder flopping idly in the waves. And there, upon her deck, were the tiny black specks of her captain and some of her crew.

The crowds had begun to disperse. The drama had come to its head. The landed Greeks were being taken away to Nauset. Nothing remained but the wrecked freighter herself.

144

And she was stuck there for a few days, stubbornly embedded into the sand. It was only at the end of the week that rescue tugs from New York managed to pull her off and escort her around to the safety of Provincetown harbor, on the first lap of her journey home.

Over that week the crowds still visited the scene. They came to look at a real shipwreck, at first hand.

But one small boy I know will always carry within him something of greater value than anyone else. He is just twelve years old, and he holds the distinction of being the very first person to swim out to that wreck and board her. He was fêted by the captain and the crew, I have been told, and given the freedom of the ship. But I like to think into the future, when the boy—himself the grandson of a sea captain—will be telling his own grandson about this wreck. By then the tale may have grown in drama. Inevitably it will become embroidered by time. But I can see, in the chain of the history of Cape Cod, one link that has been forged today by the small boy, swimming out to a wrecked freighter.

The Berry Man and Blueberry Picking

I always knew it was Manuel Enos even when he was too far away for actual recognition. He walked in a strange zigzag manner. At first I used to wonder why he did this, for most certainly he was not drunk. Then I understood: he was unable to get his highway legs. It was as though he were picking his path among bushes and undergrowth, and could not realize the unobstructed, smooth surface of the road.

Perhaps it would be more nearly right to say he walked like a hopping bird. But then, altogether he looked like a bird. His head was far too small for his body and his nose was beaked. Beneath the enormous cap he wore, with the peak pulled low over his face,

147

his black eyes sparkled with the keenness of a robin. Even his devotion to berries turned him into a queer type of bird, for you could easily imagine him pecking at the fruit with that beaklike nose.

If we are fortunate in this life we come across certain human beings with an evident aura of magic. They have little concern with worldly goods but, in common, have a special loving knowledge of their particular trade. They are usually the solitaries, whose paths run in lonely places. Sometimes one of them is a fisherman, with an awareness of the universe shown him while he sails the seas. He can be a shepherd tending his sheep alone on the Sussex Downs, or a gypsy in the mountains of Yugoslavia. I have seen him as a tramp I met in England, his entire worldly possessions upon his back, but a look of joyous magic on his unwashed face.

Manuel Enos had this same magic. And so it was that always, each time I saw him, I knew I would be enriched in my spirit.

His chief spell lay in an intimate—if unscientific—knowledge of berries. This was infused with respectful love. Blueberries, huckleberries, swamp berries, blackberries and beach plums; he knew where, from Wellfleet to Eastham on the one side, from Wellfleet to Provincetown on the other side, exactly where each could best be found that particular year.

"And the bushes just naturally get tired—just like you and me," he would tell me. "If one high bush is laden with berries this year, sure enough, next year you'll find it will be resting."

He had one worry. This was the conflict between his love for the berries and the sense that he must keep the secret of their whereabouts strictly to himself.

"It's this way," he confided to me. "You just *know* you've got to keep quiet as to where they are growing best this year. But before you can count ten, there you've gone and done it again. I

148

never mean to tell people, but I go and get all interested in thinking about the berry bushes and before I know it, by Jesus, I've told them exactly where to go and pick. And then what happens? Why, they pick every single berry off the blueberry vines and next year there aren't any. When you pick blueberries you've got to treat the bushes kindly and love them and leave some berries behind because of the seeds in them for next year. If you strip them you destroy the seeds."

Manuel Enos devoted his entire year to the berries.

"If you watch them you can see them set after the blossom comes," he went on. "I spend all my time, early in the summer, watching my bushes and seeing which one will be full. And I aim not to be foolish this year, and give away my secrets. There was a time when, if a lady was to ask me at five in the evening to get her a quart of berries, I'd have been able to go off near at hand and bring them back immediately. But now, since I've told so many folks about them, I have to go farther, and it'll take longer."

I smiled knowingly to him, for I, too, knew where I could always get some, having once been told by a Wellfleet native, who had given me the right to go to his secret places around the smaller ponds, where the high bushes still bore.

Manuel was in the mood to talk. I could not stop him.

"My mother picked berries," he went on. "She would be out by four in the morning, so she could get them before anyone saw where she went. It like makes me feel sort of soft and sad, the way I recollect how she picked, for I seem to be getting old these days and when I can get a ride I take it rather than walk. But I never lets them drive me to where exactly I wants to go. 'Let me out at such and such a corner,' I always say. And then they can think what they choose."

He winked at me, enjoying the recollection of this subterfuge.

149

That's it, I thought. The secrecy. Always the secrecy. That is really more important than the berries themselves. That is what gives the special delight and makes the sharing of this secret the highest tribute of friendship. It is the element of trespass, the triumph of pillaging, the sense of adventure in this ordered world. . . . And I was tossed back to my days of childhood, and found myself slinking along the country lanes in England with my austere old nanny, trespassing for primroses in forbidden woods. Each spring, in the search for these stolen primroses, we satisfied some urge. So, now, for me, over here in America, it may have changed from primroses to blueberries; but the need is the same, and as I go berry picking each summer with my friend Ellen and her three boys, I feel as though I am continuing the pattern of my youth. With them I become once again the child.

It is mid-July. Nobody yet says anything about it, but I notice that the old oatmeal cartons in Ellen's household are being put for safety in the corner of the woodshed. These are an essential element in our picking.

And then one day young Tom drops in to see me.

"I believe I saw old Jennie creeping along the road with her tin buckets today," he whispers.

I nod my head, knowing his meaning.

For old Jennie Poore is the forerunner of our annual ritual. It is through watching her that we know the moment for the ripening of the berries. She is the female counterpart of Manuel Enos, sharing his birdlike quality, though lacking his generosity and warmth. She is a featherless, gaunt little New England bird, sticklike and pinched. Whereas he hops along the road, she, rather, creeps.

Manuel's harvesting does not really affect us. His domain lies chiefly in the neighborhood of Bound Brook Island. It is Jennie

Poore who is our rival, for she alone knows our high bushes, hidden around the edges of old cranberry bogs and swamps. Aware that she makes a large part of her livelihood selling blueberries to the summer people, I have always a twinge of conscience when we rob her of the berries. By rights we should buy them from her, instead of gathering them ourselves.

But the seasonal urge stills my conscience. Tom has come around again to see me, and this time he pants with excitement.

"I've just seen Jennie and she had two great big buckets full—yes, brim full. And she had that special smile of hers—you know it—when she thinks she's the only one who knows where they are. Say, Clare, do you think she'll ever find out that we know?"

Getting dressed for blueberrying is tremendously important. Ellen and I have evolved a uniform, each element of which is determined by experience. To begin with, we must protect ourselves against mosquito, bramble, poison ivy and tick. This means slacks and a cotton work-shirt buttoned high to the neck and low around the wrists. And because we must wade around the oozy edges of the swamps, we wear stout shoes or boots. Our hair is tightly hidden beneath a bandana, for there are still quite a few ticks, though it is late in July. In the breast pocket of my work-shirt I have a bottle of insect repellent; mosquitoes swarm in the wet, low-lying bogs. Elaborately I anoint myself before I start, till I begin to be afraid lest my blueberries will taste of the horrid liquid; but it seems to have little effect, for during the afternoon the mosquitoes' ping sounds loud in my ears. Remembering the time I lost the key of the car from the pocket of my shirt, when I stumbled over a tree stump, I secure it these days with an enormous safety pin.

We are ready. Even before we start we feel distressingly hot.

"Regular blueberrying weather," says Tom. "Never known

it to fail. The day might start out chilly, but once you and Mum make up your minds to go, it gets steamy and hot. Never known it to fail."

"This is nothing," I laugh. "Wait till we actually get picking."

If only we could go in our ordinary summer clothes, with our skin exposed, it would be so much more comfortable. But we know very well why both Manuel and Jennie cover themselves. We, too, have been scratched and stung.

The three boys rush out to the car, laden with the old circular oatmeal cartons. This is the first year Robbie is old enough to pick, though actually you could say that he came with us that summer, four years ago, before he was born. Ellen was heavy with carrying him, and the two boys and I pulled down the topmost branches of the bushes, in a "Cherry Tree" carol atmosphere of reverence, so that Ellen would not have to stretch high.

But time has passed, and Robbie clambers now into the car with his own small-size oatmeal carton. This year he intends to pick.

The boys have strung the cartons ready, with old rags, that we may hang them around our necks. Never again will we use string. We have learnt our lesson; as the cartons grew heavy, filled with the blueberries, the string had cut deep into our skin.

And then the ritual begins. There is a strange sense of security in a secret understanding, whatever it may be. So each summer, as we find ourselves using our particular expressions about the blueberry picking, a bond strengthens around us. Robbie has already learned them.

"Is your bottom covered yet?" the baby pipes up, when we have been picking for some time.

Ellen and I chuckle. Over the years of our picking together we have asked each other this, boastfully proclaiming that we have already picked so many blueberries that no longer can we see the bare base of the oatmeal carton.

"Jennie's beaten us to it again," the two older boys shout, as we dive into the thicket to our secret blueberry patch. "The tall grasses have been trampled down into a narrow path. She's been here before us."

"Not so loud," we hush them. "Not so much noise, else people might hear us."

We slink through the grasses, charged with a sense of secrecy. I believe we would never have enjoyed this ritual half as much had we felt safe. I shall never know what special specter of danger loomed in front of the others, but I do know that always I saw that fantastically tall gamekeeper in England, looking down upon a crouching child as she stole primroses in a forbidden wood.

Tommy finds it hard to keep quiet.

"Quick," he shouts to us. "Come this way. Don't bother about your piddling bushes. I've found a virgin bush of blues. Yes, it's a real virgin bush. I think it must have grown too tall for Jennie."

I smile. Here he is, again, with our secret sayings.

We scramble towards him, highly critical of the blueberries we leave unpicked. For we know each bush—the high blacks that are pippy and apt to crinkle in the heat of summer, the special wide large blues that have so many deep pinks among them when they ripen. There are the darker, flatter blues, with a smoky bloom to them; and the smaller blues that spot their branches in twos and threes; the ancient bushes that bear the tougher, skimpier berries; and then, finally, the young bush we come upon unexpectedly, with its half-hidden clumps of berries that are so tender and full. We know them all, the lows and the highs that soar so much above the others that we can scarcely reach them, but jump in the air to secure the branches and hold them down while the others pick.

"I remember a marvelous blue around the next curve of the swamp," I say, though I was away in England the year before and it has been two summers since last I picked. My visual memory knows that special bush. It has not been blurred by a season of absence. "And it ought to be heavily laden today, for two years back it was thick with berries and I am sure, as Manuel would say, it must have rested last season."

"Are you milking yet?" I call then to Ellen.

"No," she answers. "Not yet. It's just ones and twos."

We have to work up to the rhythm of picking. At first we are tentative, pulling off a few berries here and there. We hear the brittle plop of the blueberries falling upon the empty base of the carton. Soon that brittle plop grows muted as our "bottoms are covered." Jealously, with a sense of friendly rivalry, we listen for the tell-tale sounds of each other's picking.

And then the fever consumes us. We milk down into the cartons. Gently we enfold these full bunches of ripe berries within the clasp of our hands; then with a little tug we detach them from their stems. The oatmeal cartons grow heavier with each minute, till we have to pause and empty them into paper bags.

"Oh, look," I whisper as we finally decided to stop, in this steamy heat. "Look along there. I see it—a very special bush— a bush I don't even seem to remember."

By now we are so excited that we begin to pick with less care, pulling whole clusters of blueberries into the cartons, regardless of whether they are ripe. I glance down and see twigs and leaves and green berries tossed in among the ripe ones. The passion has us now in its grip.

The hours pass as we pick. Robbie is tired and we have put him to rest under a bush, on a bed of soft grass. Peter is bored, but little Tom is valiant still. Tom, though, begins soon to falter.

154

"Let's go, Mum," he urges with sudden fretfulness.

But Ellen and I still pick. We creep along to the edge of the next swamp, fringed with its horrid, sun-warmed muck. Our feet sink deep into ooze, which fills our shoes. When we drag our feet up out of it, we hear a sugging sound, as of the tide that sucks against a wharf. Enormous frogs, scarcely distinguishable from this mud, with bright green faces the color of the water grasses and weeds, and with gold glints to their eyes, squat immobile, staring at us intruders. We tickle them with a grass and they jump with the alacrity of a thought, into the edge of the water. They are followed by the leaps of countless tiny frogs. This is a primordial scene, steamy with heat, a fierce sun blazing down upon us and the ceaseless ping of mosquitoes in our ears.

"Why do we do all this?" I ask suddenly. "We could go and buy these berries for practically nothing and avoid the heat and mud and mosquito bites, and the scratches and the exhaustion of this sun that drenches us with sweat and makes us almost dizzy. Why are we so foolish . . . ?"

We laugh, knowing we shall do it again next summer; for we are slaves to a ritual. We do not dare to deny the power of this ritual.

The sun lowers in the summer sky. We are still picking. Viciously the mosquitoes sting, for once I am caught up into the frenzy of the gathering I forget to dab myself with insect repellent. The sense of urgency consumes me—a needless, grotesque urgency, for the bushes will stay here till we have picked. They will be here long after we are dead. Why do we rush? What force drives us? Why, in fact, do we do this . . . ?

Then, just as we have decided to leave, we remember certain specially full-bearing low bushes along the far edge of the pond.

But we are balked. These low-bush berries adjoined a deserted house. This year we find that summer people have rented the place. A line of swim suits dries in front of the old house by the water's edge. Beyond this, we know, lie the bountiful low bushes, loaded with ripe berries. We cannot reach them.

Our disproportionate grief turns to amusement.

"Let's call it a day," I shout, hoping the new summer people will hear. "Let's just go."

But one final element in our ritual remains unfulfilled. We are hot from the swampy heat and creeping, probably, with ticks.

"You keep a lookout," we tell the boys. "We're going to have our swim, and don't let anyone come near."

And then we two women shed our clothing. Sticky from picking, we plunge into the cool water of the little pond, as we have done over many years. Recklessly we fling ourselves among the water lilies, knowing that three small boys keep watch.

Driving home with the tired children and the blueberries in brown paper bags and old oatmeal cartons, we sit high with the pride of those who have dared idiotically to surrender to an urge. Before us lies the prospect of tedious hours in a hot kitchen, where Ellen and I will put up the berries for the winter. But the blueberries in themselves matter little, though we shall, undoubtedly, boast of them to city friends over the months of winter as we bring out the sealed jars for special occasions. What we really have gained is something intangible but of great value; we have made our offering to the gods who demand the service of ritual.

And now as I write this I feel a sadness, for I have just learned that Jennie is dead. Never again shall we see the little birdlike figure creeping along the sand paths with her tin buckets, a smile of secret triumph upon her face. Neither shall we know any longer the precise moment when the blueberries are ready for picking. For we are now the sole custodians of those particular bushes that grow thickly around the edge of the disused cranberry bog.

But this sadness about Jennie has been deepened for me by another happening. Manuel, the Portuguese berry man, has grown so old and infirm that he is no longer able to come around.

So they pass, these two lovers of berries. They had a constant devotion to the berries, above and beyond the fact that they were their livelihood. You had only to see the glow on Manuel Enos's face when he talked about beach plums to know you were in the presence of an artist, a man touched by God.

"If there's anything on earth more beautiful than the foaming white of the beach plum in bloom," he had told me one day, "if there's anything you can name that beats it, just you tell me. And to think that all that white foamy stuff—all that blossoming— isn't just like the foam on the waves at the back shore that means nothing. It's what's going to fade and drift away and set into plums —all pale green and then pink and then deep purple-blue—just like all sorts of little rainbows. Beautiful, they are. Just beautiful. And then, as well as looking so beautiful, think how they taste. Why, some of them—if you can find the really big, ripe ones— some of them taste so good you can eat them raw."

He loved them. He really loved his berries. And so, too, did little old Jennie. Those two belonged with all harvesters through the ages, whether of the olive or the grape in the Mediterranean, the apple, the wheat or the corn. For they carried within themselves, in those puny, thin, little birdlike bodies, the sense of wonder.

"It's going to be pretty hard to have to try to live up to Jennie and Manuel," I told myself. Then, thinking suddenly of the impersonal, commercial harvests of today, I found myself adding: "And not only hard, but very important."

Dogwood, or
A Matter of Semantics

And what, you might well ask, has this got to do with Cape Cod? I would have asked the same thing, before this past summer. But I chanced to suffer greatly because of that word "semantics," which means the meaning of a word.

It all began with the time when I got stung by a jellyfish.

It happens that I am one of those unfortunate creatures called allergics. Everything that stings me, from a bee upwards, makes me violently sick.

I was swimming in the Bay of Cape Cod one day in July, enjoying myself as much as anyone has probably ever done. I never even had the satisfaction of seeing the actual jellyfish that stung me. I had been warned that the excessive heat of this particular summer had carried them further north than usual—these jelly-fish that would normally have stayed in the Chesapeake Bay. And I do know that over at the back shore, on the Atlantic, I had seen quantities of them, deposited at low tide upon the sands. They are beautiful, though evil-looking, transparent and streaked with deep brown like a prune whip that has gone all floppy. I had looked down upon these circular messes, admiring the aesthetic ingenuity of Nature. But never had I supposed they portended me evil. Neither had I imagined they would have come around the point of Provincetown to the relative seclusion of the bay, where every-thing seemed so safe.

"If I swim over here," I had told myself, remembering my susceptibilities, "if I don't go over to the back side until the jellyfish have left, I'll be all right."

But a special jellyfish must have been destined to lie in wait for me. Just a day or two after one of the most delicious swims I can remember, I saw an inexplicable red patch on my thigh, below the edge of my swim suit. The red patch expanded, and I was very sick. I lay in bed for many days as the poison spread from this local area and—during an unprecedented heat wave—came out all over me, on chest and stomach, arms and legs, in violent scarlet that itched like twenty devils.

The local inhabitants were worried. They didn't like this to have happened. They seemed to feel a queer shame, as though it were their responsibility.

Perhaps it wasn't really an ordinary jellyfish, they said, trying to clear their consciences with regard to the water surrounding their Cape. Perhaps it was a stray octopus, or a Portuguese man-of-war? Who knows? Perhaps it was even dogwood?

But no, I told them, vaguely wondering why they should men-tion dogwood as a suspect. Definitely it was a jellyfish.

162

It was this event that set the stage for what happened later that year. Always the inhabitants kept on warning me about the dogwood. You must be careful of the dogwood, they would say. Don't you—of all people, not you—don't ever go anywhere near it, not within half a mile, if you can help it. You've no idea what it can do to you.

And I remembered, then, how Manuel Enos, the Portuguese berry man, had talked to me about this legendary dogwood.

"By Jesus," he would warn me. "If you get the berry of the dogwood on you it hurts like the son of a gun. It's all right, perhaps, if you've got specially good blood in you, but otherwise, by Jesus, it burns like the devil."

Dogwood, I had then reflected. No one had ever told me that the beautiful dogwood tree was evil. And then I began to think further. Somehow, I had never even seen a dogwood tree up here on Cape Cod. Coming from England, I had seen it first in Maryland. I had lived with it for nearly ten years in North Carolina, enjoying its blanket of snow in early spring, against the violent color of the redbud tree. Actually, as I came more to think about it, one of the things I had really missed here on the Cape, when I had left the South, was the dogwood. Then why did they keep on warning me about it?

As they continued to tell me of its dangers—remembering my distressing time with the jellyfish poisoning—I kept on searching for even one single dogwood tree.

"It's just nonsense," I laughed to myself. "They're trying to scare me. They are giving themselves a wonderful time trying to make me think there are all sorts of things around here that I must be afraid of."

But the moment came when I knew better.

It was the end of September. Most of the flowers on Cape Cod were over. I needed something with which to decorate my house. Surely I could find some autumn leaves? And anyhow, I needed to go to the town dump. On my way there, I knew, I would find some foliage. Only, *I must beware of dogwood.*

I did. I never saw one single dogwood tree—not the dogwood as I have learnt to know it. But, as I came away from the dump, I chanced, alas, to look towards my right. There, below the railroad tracks in the swampy meadows, flamed some brilliantly crimson bushes. They were not dogwood. Of that I felt certain. I went closer, and saw that they were a variety of sumac.

Now I have picked sumac many times in my life. Living in Connecticut, I have cut great branches of the bush, with its decorative bronze-crimson seed pods. This particular sumac seemed more delicate and refined. It bore the same kind of leaves, but they were much less coarse than the ones I had known. I got out of the car, and gathered an armful of the crimson foliage. I bore it home, knowing I would have something startlingly beautiful in my living room.

That day I forgot all about this fantastic dogwood myth.

But next day was something very different. My wrists suddenly began to itch. I looked at them and noticed, to my distress, that there were clumps of red spots all over my skin.

"They're nothing," I laughed. "They're only the rough places where I tore against the branches."

But I was wrong.

These spots began to swell. My face began to swell. My eyes disappeared from sight and, beneath my chin, I grew a beard of muck and ooze. I had never supposed a human being could look so revolting.

This went on for two or three weeks. When I had to go to town to buy my food, I draped myself in scarves and wore colored

164

glasses. But nobody who has not endured this particular torment could know how I was feeling. It was about fifty times worse than an excessively bad attack of poison ivy. Doctors tended me, and a really true, loving friend dressed my repulsive looking, oozing arms.

And then a strange compensation happened. In the oddest of ways this filthy allergic poisoning made me belong to the Cape as had nothing else before. I had lived here over many years, and been practically accepted. But something very subtly was lacking, and this fulfilled that need.

"Dogwood," said the oldest inhabitant, as he passed me outside the post office. "You poor thing, you've been up against the dogwood."

"It'll last two or three weeks, at the very least," said another fisherman, as he sighed on beholding me. "There's just nothing you can do but wait. I've had it. We've all had it. I was pretty near blinded by it for almost one month. Nothing as you can do but wait."

"And my husband was in the hospital with it," said someone else. "Nearly lost the sight of his eyes."

"It's dogwood. It's dogwood. It's dogwood."

In my state of intense misery I didn't really mind what it was. But somewhere at the back of my mind I had a sense of confused, resentful amusement.

Why did they need to call it dogwood? It was really a sumac.

If they'd only given it the right name I would have watched out for it, and this horrible thing would never have happened.

I got well. One always does. It took an ungodly time. And never have I suffered more. But one thing has come out of it. I now belong to Cape Cod. It is sad that one must suffer so to belong. But that's the truth of the matter. And I know now that every time I see the oldest inhabitant here in Wellfleet, or meet the most ancient fisherman, they will yearn over me with compassion, as I recall to their minds the vision of this revolting spectacle last fall, swathed in rags, covered with bandages, oozing and sore and in pain. And they will gather me into their midst, yet one more human being who has had an encounter with the dogwood.

After all, what does it really matter now what that accursed bush is called? I have served my apprenticeship and I know I belong.

The Rituals of Summer

Each June, when school got out, my neighbor friends arrived. Then we began our summer rituals together. Life was filled with the many little things that must be done if the pattern of the year were rightly to be fulfilled.

And because the family included three young boys, there was a constant sense of the wonder of life—that wonder which dims as we reach adulthood but which can illuminate the world.

I lived, with them, the inevitable "firsts" of the season: the first visit to the bay, the first swim, the first sight of the ocean. The

Cape, then, in early summer, held an especial clarity of light, imparting a first-day-of-Creation feeling, like the opening movement of Beethoven's Ninth Symphony. The leaves of the honey locusts shone yellow-green in the sun against the clean blue of the sky. Everything so brimmed with youth that it held the power to peel back the years and restore the excitements of childhood to us older persons. The heat of summer had not yet tired the countryside; meadows were white with daisies, yellow with coreopsis, purple with vetch. The dunes glowed golden with poverty grass in bloom. Little white boats tossed on the bay, shining in their new coats of paint. This moment of clear joy was preciously transient. It would never more exist until the following June.

The first general ritual of the year, controlled by impersonal timing, was the annual Blessing of the Fleet, in Provincetown. This was followed by the bonfire and fireworks on the Fourth of July. We watched this always from the little cove at the bottom of our road, with fireworks and stars doubled in the water. Robbie, the youngest boy, stayed up late for the event, enchanting us with his diminutive, Promethean magic as he caught the stars and fireworks in his tiny hands and presented them to us, delicately and guardedly, secure in the belief that he held within those little hands stars of silver and gold from the midnight sky.

After that came the annual blueberry gathering, with its elaborate rituals. This merged into the picking of water lilies from our secret lily pond.

We drive along the narrow sand roads through the woods, the sweet pepper bushes and bay swishing against the car. Down below, through breaks in these bushes, we can see the chain of bright blue ponds. But our particular lily pond is none of these. It is a hidden one, and—we like to believe—known to nobody but us.

Our pond is never blue like the others. It is covered with algae

168

and scum. If you look down into its depths, it is like a three-dimensional world of pond life, in horizontal layers of vegetation.

What hazards abound in picking water lilies. Some years it is simpler than others, for then the pond is shrunken in size and we can walk along the edge, upon dry land. But at other times, even in a season of extreme heat and drought, the pond is bigger than usual, swollen from early spring rains. And then we have to wade around it, in all the slime and muck.

We go to this pond always in the morning, while still the water lilies are opened wide. The sun glistens on the surface scum in a quiver of light. It is like a painting by a French Impressionist. I find myself thinking of Monet as I sweep aside the heavy bushes that protect the pond from vulgar view and see the sparkle of water on the flat green plates of lily pads. There, all along the edge of the pond, squat the little frogs. Their gold eyes catch this morning sunlight, till, as I glance towards them, it is almost like the signaling of countless heliographs. Rich, deep gold is held within the eyes of these bright green frogs.

And then, as I look around me, I see a thick patterning of the pretty, tiny, pink water orchids, and the green spearing arrow-heads which are the young leaves of the water hyacinths, pointing upright out of this scummy pond. We follow the fringe of the pond, treading upon the thick wet softness of cranberry vines. Before us when we tread, frogs hop across our path, from the cool little green caves in the depth of this foliage. As they plop into the pond they make spreading, overlapping circles upon the surface of the water.

"Better not take off our shoes," Ellen and I say each year, knowing how much we want to feel this cool thick growth beneath the soles of our bare feet. "Remember there are supposed to be blood suckers in this pond. And they are frightening things."

169

For we never forget that one of these ponds, not far from ours, carries the name of Horse Leech Pond.

And so, while ashamed of our cowardice, we keep on our sneakers when we go water-lily picking.

The flowers seem always to grow just beyond our reach.

"One of these days we'll have to get hold of a tiny collapsible boat," I suggest. "Then we can go far out and find the best and biggest of the water lilies." But in the meantime we must invade this horrible slime, scared of what we may come up against as we wade further into the pond, away from the edge.

Low in the air around me, like a fugue of flight, I see the dragonflies: sapphire-blue darning needles everywhere, thin and clear, delicate as gauze; large, gray-blue dragonflies, resting on lily pads and on the white flowers themselves; and the huge russet-orange ones, of the color of a wood thrush. The dragonflies hover and dart, smooth yet abrupt in their manner of flight, so swift of movement that their wings are invisible. As I look down into the pond, between the clumps of algae where the water is clear, I see tiny fish, with their shadows beneath them, darting in the same rhythm of movement as that of the flight of the dragonflies. The stagnant, static world of the lily pond is threaded with life.

We have to wade far out, till the water is halfway up our thighs. Like little girls paddling at the ocean's edge, we have tucked our skirts high, into our belts.

"I've got the first one," calls Ellen, as she holds a lily high in the air, the long red-brown stem hanging limply down like a water snake. "And there are heaps of them further along—if only I dare go there."

The bottom of the pond is squelchy and slimy. I do not know upon what I tread. I feel insecure, as though I might at any moment step into a quicksand and vanish beneath the surface.

170

The sun is high in the sky, and the lilies are still wide open. Drops of water glisten on their petals, which have an artificial quality of cold perfection as though they were made of flawless china, or modeled in wax. Even the yellow of their stamens seems

false. I need to get close to one of them, that its subtle perfume may assure me it is a plant and not an exotic, man-made work of art.

Soon, as the afternoon passes, these flowers of visionary whiteness will close for the night and become, until the sunlight of tomorrow opens them once more, tight, creamy-green buds.

We wade back to dry land, our legs covered with filthy slime and scum. But my hands are filled with lilies and I am satisfied.

Each summer must hold for me a bowl of these water lilies.

Then, as the year passes, and the limbs of the children turn brown in the sun, bringing a tough growth to their young bodies, the beach plums ripen in this same hot sun. And a mood of secrecy enfolds us as we go out once again to gather fruit. It is the same secrecy that surrounds us at the time of blueberry picking. Nobody can wrench from us the knowledge of where the best beach plums can be found, though this is the most important harvest of the year, stripping the stores of their supply of sugar and glass jars as the fever of jelly-making consumes the women of the Cape.

The season of extreme heat is here, bringing warm nights, beach picnics and clambakes. This means swimming after dark without the clutter of a swim suit, when no one can see us. We walk down the sand paths, the enormous stars shining bright behind the scrubby pines. For some reason or other, the bay shore is always deserted. Even at the highest point of the season, when the Cape is filled with summer visitors, you will find the beaches empty of people. It is as though mankind has not learnt the beauty of the night. Along the back shore, on the ocean side, you will see occasional rosy gleams from the driftwood fires of beach picnics, where close little groups clump together into late evening. But on the bay side, or around the ponds, everything is black and still.

There is nothing blacker than black water at night. I dive into a pond, wondering if I shall be able to find my way to shore. All directions and dimensions have been lost in darkness. There is neither left nor right, above nor below, for even the water confuses me with the doubling of the stars from the sky upon its surface. Only the branches of pine trees, blotting out these stars, guide me back to land. Night water feels especially wet. One can surrender to it more completely than during the daytime when the mind is diffused and obstructed by the sense of sight. This, I suppose, must be the intensity of feeling of the man who is blind, and his compensation for the loss of one of his senses.

I swim at night in the ocean. It is black all around, and only by the dim frilly edging of white foam at the tide line can I determine where the sea begins. Farther out, the milky colored waves break in rhythmic thumps. Every subtle sound of the ocean is heightened by darkness. I can almost believe I hear the sand itself shifting. . . . There are no stars this night in the sky, but I am secured in my place on the planet by the red and green lights of passing fishing boats and the steady, flashing yellow gleam from a lightship on the horizon. To the north the blackness is broken by a regular stroking flash from the Highland Light, assuring and benign, like a protecting arm of pale gold.

But there is a special wonder to be experienced only very rarely, and then unexpectedly. It would seem that it must happen during extreme heat. It is what has been called the luminous tides. Then, on these magical nights, you find the surf shining silver with phosphorescence. Plunge into the sea and you swim in sparkling silver. Fling the water over your body and you are drenched in these glistening jewels. It is living silver, supposedly composed of a mass of bacterial life. The experience carries the quality of a fairy tale. One feels like the enchanted princess, in this flooding of silver light.

Summer passes, and the specter of leaving tosses its shadow before it. The children begin to count the days to their departure. A thin streak of sadness enters into our rituals. No longer is it a matter of the "first" time of doing something or going somewhere. Now it is always "we must do this and that, before we leave."

We must have our annual picnic at the mouth of the Pamet River, carefully watching the time of the tides lest we get trapped there and cannot return. We must visit the Highland Light, and

173

Thumpertown Beach. We must—oh, but the plans crowd each other so thickly that we know many of them will remain unfulfilled.

A final harvesting beckons us. It is a utilitarian harvesting, though it holds the same delight as blueberrying and beach-plum gathering. The moment has come for the ripening of the choke cherry. Along the back roads these graceful trees that, like the honey locusts, belong to the world of the French artist Claude Lorrain, these delicate-leaved trees drip their black clusters of wild cherries.

Ellen and I make a jelly from these cherries that is richer and more prized than any that could be made from the beach plum. It is incomparable eaten with meat. We also make that delectable drink called cherry bounce.

Once again we bring out our oatmeal cartons. Once more we milk the fruit down into them.

And then, when the jelly has been made, and the specially large, perfect cherries have been selected for the bounce, the shelf in my kitchen, facing the sun, will hold a stand of bottles, filled with cherries, rum and sugar, to "work" in this sun, evidence of the passing of the summer.

It seems now as though almost all the undeniable annual rituals have been performed. And that is as it must be, for only a little while remains before the knell of Labor Day.

Our final celebration is always the supper on the back shore. As I think of this now, I remember one particular beach picnic that was filled with special enchantment.

It was about a month before Robbie was to be born, and his mother was heavy with the burden of the child. The date for the picnic had been set, but when the day arrived it was dreary and cold. Early in the evening we drove to the back shore, to see

174

whether we could possibly find shelter for the celebration. As we reached the ocean we saw the great wild beauty of the place. The waves were big and white and very rough, and the gray sky was windy and threatened rain.

"It's far too cold," we women told each other as we walked briskly along the beach to keep warm. But the two small boys and

a friend of mine who had been included in the picnic were running before us with delight.

"Let's get together some logs," called Tom. And we gathered smooth, silver-gray driftwood—great logs of trees that must have been carried out to sea off the coast of Maine, spruce stripped of their bark with gawky bare limbs sticking out at all angles, big trunks of trees that seemed too big for any man to lift and carry.

In this cold, dreary, windy evening, I became aware that I was being whirled into a ritual that surmounted the weather. A ceremony was being acted out. The two boys and my friend Paul collected twigs and dug a hole in the sand. All around this tiny hole they massed branches and logs and pieces of wood as a windbreak.

And then the first thin flame showed. The fire had been started. It was the little Tom who seemed to understand that you dare not deny a ritual. We women were timid of the cold and the wind and the possible rain. But he held the insight of the child.

"Let's have our supper down here, after all," he stated. "We MUST make a fire. We simply must. We always do."

Gradually the wisdom of the small child entered into us. We left the menfolk here on the beach, Ellen and I, and went back home to prepare supper. We acted like crazy women, controlled by some power outside of ourselves as we packed hot soup for the thermos bottles, bread and cheese, olives and peaches. I found my last bottle of red wine, which I had kept for "a most special occasion." We returned to the back shore, the car stuffed with blankets and leather coats, against the cold.

When we reached the menfolk at last, we saw that they had been busy while we were away. And one of the first strokes of magic touched me as I thought of this unstated, instinctive division of labor: we, the women, concerning ourselves with the food and they, the men, gathering the great logs for the fire to keep us warm.

Everyone looked bewitched, taking on the qualities of a legend. The shadows and the caprice of the firelight gave an aura of magic. As the grown man stood there on the beach, the ends of his woolen scarf waving loose in the wind, the tall staff of a tree in one hand, ready to stir the fire, he looked like some primitive Greek or Highland shepherd tending his sheep. What did it matter that here, tonight, the sheep were mere hillocks of sand, around his feet?

The fire grew stronger as dusk began to fall. We unpacked the food and settled ourselves upon an especially big log the men-

176

folk had placed for us in the warmth of the driftwood fire.

The night thickened and enclosed us as we ate until we, this little clump of human beings—Ellen, thinking of her unborn baby; quiet, serious little Peter; the dramatic, vibrant little Vulcan, Tom, with such grace in his movements as he stoked the fire and became, in his mind, the tender of all the fire in the whole world; and my friend Paul—we were in a charmed circle, separated from the outside world.

Each one of us, sitting there, watching the great flames as they leapt and danced and consumed the silver driftwood, was aware that this was a space of magic, precious in its rarity.

"We'll never forget this fire and this evening," said little Tom, with great seriousness in his voice. "Never, I say. We'll remember it, all the winter long, always."

There is one allegiance in life we dare not deny. It is to the unsought moment of enchantment. Then, at that moment, on the edge of the Atlantic, the spell was so strong that it held the power to turn a passing vessel on the horizon, showing dimly in the deepening dusk, into a *Flying Dutchman*, Moby Dick's ship towing the White Whale, a transatlantic liner—anything rather than a mere fishing boat.

Complete darkness fell before we quite knew it. And the sparks from the tended fire grew brighter each minute. The flame in the heart of the fire was pale yellow, crocus-yellow, pink, scarlet, crimson. Little veins of fierce crimson ran along the half-burnt logs as they lay across the fire. The stark branches of the spruce caught aflame and blazed. And as we went on sitting there, into the night with darkness around us, the shape of the dunes faintly visible in the glow from our fire and in the regular, stroking light from the far-off Highland Light, alternately brilliant and reflected, like the systolic-diastolic beat of the bloodstream, as we sat there we knew, each one of us, that we battled with time. The minutes were passing, even as the great logs shifted and fell into the heart of the flames, even as they grew smaller and were consumed.

Then, as it were in a desperate effort to conquer time and make this moment of quiet ecstasy endure, the man would get up and vanish into the darkness, searching for more driftwood. Again and again he carried great gray trunks upon his shoulders and flung them into the fire.

"Oh, let this fire go on and on," I wanted to call into the night. "Don't let this moment slip away, for it will never return."

Across our faces, from the incoming tide, came a sprinkle of spindrift. Or was it the threatened rain? We neither knew nor cared. We were drugged with delight. And always there, if we should stop our minds from turning to each other or watching the fire, always in the background was the thumping of the waves in the strong wind.

It must have been several hours that we sat so, scarcely speaking. Occasionally the man slipped away into the darkness to collect more logs. It was an unavailing struggle with time.

For we knew that once we left this place the magic would be shattered.

"Good-bye, Cape Cod," came the tired voice of little Tom, as we carried him across the sands to the car. "See you again next year."

As we left, we turned to the sea. The moon was breaking through the clouds; its path upon the sea was like silver satin, creased and crumpled by the wind.

And, as though we were almost ashamed of this momentary touching upon something magical, out and beyond us, we were silent in the darkness all the way home.

Next day, in the harsh light of morning, the boys brought up their boats from the bay. Into the woodshed they placed them for the winter—Peter's small sailboat and *Tom Kat*, the little skiff that Tommy had saved up his money to buy. Labor Day was upon the family, with its ruthless, arbitrary division of the seasons. Irrevocably, summer had ended.

Dredging the Harbor

How quickly I have forgotten what the place looked like before the harbor was dredged and the wharf was built. I thought I would remember forever the exact line of that shore. I even believed I knew each curve of sand and the precise shape of every rock. I had spent so many years there, walking and swimming, or helping the fishermen bring in the oysters and clams. I had watched that shore line at high tide and low tide, in winter and summer, till I supposed the image was so imprinted upon my mind that I would be able to draw an exact picture of it to the end of my life.

I hate change. I used to hate change even in the garden of my childhood, in England, when my father decided to make a new flower bed or cut down a tree. "Oh, do you really *need* to do that?" I would plead to him. "Won't you leave it as it is . . . ?"

I cannot justify this dread of change. It must be mere female sentimentality, for life perpetually and inevitably changes. When it related to the building of the new dock I should have been able to ignore my dislike of change, for I had been one of the dock's staunchest supporters. Over some time I had been worried as I watched the town being caught up into the unhealthy pattern of a summer resort. It must be turned back to the fishermen, to whom by rights it belonged.

So, with my intelligence and with all the integrity within me, I rejoiced when the dredgers came.

Their arrival was well timed. The last summer visitor had left. The sand upon the shore was smooth, unpitted by anything more disturbing than the delicate footprints of sandpiper or gull. Gone were the clumps of sun bathers and swimmers, beneath their brightly colored beach umbrellas. The coastline was so deserted and silent that it seemed strange to have this sudden invasion of machinery.

The first hint we had about these happenings came from Jesse Medeiros. He had been warned to move his oyster beds. I went down with him each day, scooming in the black mud of low tide.

This old oysterman had conflict within him. Nobody more vehemently wanted to bring the town back to its honest, rightful heritage than Jesse Medeiros. By rights he should unconfusedly have rejoiced, but he, too, seemed to feel a sentimental sadness at the prospect of change.

"I know it's got to happen," he said as we cleaned up the oyster beds. "I know it. I know it. And yet somehow I wish it could have been done without my having to lose my beds."

Oh, but that's it, I wanted to comfort him. Don't you know you've got to pay for everything?

"I've had these beds here ever since I was a boy," he went on. "And my father before me. If it hadn't been for the summer people we could have managed all right."

I smiled, for I knew perfectly well that he was aware that what was happening was far beyond the power of mere city folks. The

182

steady silting up of the harbor and the changing of our shore line resulted from the same force of the tides that had submerged the island of Billingsgate and made it today nothing but a buoy-marked danger to fishermen. It was the same force that had reduced the harbor of Truro to a muddy inlet and made Rock Harbor at Orleans practically useless. The changing coastline was something independent of man.

And then they came. Two enormous crimson dredgers arrived, filled with strangers. One of them came right up into the channel within Shirttail Point, anchoring there to house the workers. And with this arrival there developed an odd, feverish quiver of disquieting excitement, as though foreign birds had invaded our territory.

Even the efficiency of these professionals confused us. Twenty-four hours a day they worked, in tireless shifts. The indigo night of our autumn skies was a backdrop to the garish lights of the dredger.

"Just like a drugstore out at sea," grumbled Jesse. "Nothing on earth but a lighted up drugstore that has lost its way."

"Even more like a calliope, a paddle steamer on the Mississippi," I thought. And I kept on expecting to hear the jangle of music from *Showboat*.

How completely they did take over. They felt no sentiment about us. They were unaware of the complexity of our emotions. But then, we ourselves scarcely knew what we were confusedly feeling.

"It's good. It's right. It's what had to happen," we all told each other, without actually saying the words.

None of us seemed able to tear ourselves from the scene. I believe we felt we were custodians of this shore line, and stayed there to see that nothing wrong was done. Or perhaps we merely wanted to watch this alien activity, as mankind gathers always before any machinery. All the day long the wooden benches by the shore—those benches that were filled throughout the summer months with vacationists—all through the hours, the benches were occupied with watching fishermen.

"How does it really feel, having strangers come in and take over in your waters?" I asked.

"Oh, well," they answered. "We just sit and watch."

And that is exactly what they did.

And now a chain of strange little boats fanned out into the bay, surveying the scene and testing the depth of the channel. The next thing we knew, these boats had been changed—or were they something else? I shall never know—into a curved pontoon causeway, supporting the discharge pipe, and this great pipe, like a gigantic sea serpent, began then to belch forth filthy black muck upon the beach. It was strange stuff, filled with the smell of the depths of the ocean, unholy, primordial, charged with such sulphurous power that it chemically blackened the paint on the surface of the white beach house.

I don't think many of us in Wellfleet did much work that week of the dredging. I know I didn't. From the windows of my house I could look down over the bay and watch the operations. I cooked to this, and washed my dishes to it. And then, whenever I could, I rushed down to the beach. Always at any time of the day, the shore was crowded with fishermen.

The evil-smelling black mud spurted out. It was like the blood of the ocean, being drained from its body. I found myself almost wanting to staunch this wound, it was so dreadful. So it's like this, I thought. All the hidden life at the bed of the sea is black—black, deprived of oxygen and light. The mud rattled with pebbles and broken oyster shells. Within it must be untold wonders of submarine life. One expected surely to see some signs of this life, some minute fish, at the very least; but it was dead, and it gave one the feeling of being the deadest thing on the earth.

It seemed all wrong to have it scooped up and exposed thus. Was this what we all came from, in the remotest past? Did I gaze upon the beginning of life on this planet?

I switched my mind from these conjectures and began prosaically to think of the actual black muck. Our beach, I supposed, would be spoiled for ever. Who could possibly walk over this filth? Who would dare to lie upon it in the sun?

One of the fishermen must have guessed my thoughts, for he turned to me.

"It won't take long before that black stuff will be just like the sand that was here before," he assured me. "Let the sun and the light get to it and it'll be purified and bleached white."

That's it, I supposed. It's because it was hidden away from the light. This is an example of the power of light and the power of the sun.

Actually, even at the end of a day or two the black filth had started to change. As it dried in the sun it took on a faint silvery sheen and lost a great deal of its mood of evil. I dared even to walk upon it. Perhaps the old fisherman might be right? I still couldn't entirely believe him, though I did notice that the blackened beach house had begun to return to its original white.

As the great pipe belched this muck, changes were taking place in the shore itself. A channel was being cut down into the mud, coming nearer and nearer to the shore line and the new dock. Low tide, until this time, had been a desolate stretch of mud. Now, as the tide went out, a river of water appeared, dark, in the banks of the rest of the mud. Before our eyes was the source of this belched muck. We could see what was actually happening.

All this while piles were being driven into the water's edge further around, for the new dock. As I watched, I began to feel once again the familiar dread of change. When we have the wharf, jutting far enough into deep water so that the boats can anchor against it, when this has happened, I know, it will be wonderful and right for the fishermen. They will no longer have to anchor out in the bay and transfer their quahogs and scallops into the dories. But, then, I questioned suddenly with a shock, as my qualms took shape, but then will the need for the dory disappear? And I looked across at the dredger and the black muck to the far side of the shore line, to the delicate shaped, incomparably beautiful dories, bobbing on the water at high tide, and I remembered how lovely they look, too, at low tide, lying in the sand on their sides, like stranded fish or small white whales or even sleeping birds. And a great love for these little boats welled up within me. It was a love infused with respect, for I had tried to draw them so often and each time I had been increasingly aware of the subtlety of their form. I thought then of all little boats I had ever known—rowboats in England, tiny boats in the Adriatic with orange-colored butterfly sails, and the gondolas of Venice with the strange twist to their structure. I thought next of my young friend Tommy and the little white skiff he had bought the past summer with money earned over a paper route and several winters of shoveling snow. I had been present at the ceremonial launching and christening of the skiff, and had seen the boy row out alone across the bay, *Tom Kat* doubled in the smooth water, the splash of the oars glistening in the sun.

There it is again, I thought. You gain one thing but you lose another. And I felt that here, looking upon the dredging of our harbor, I was witnessing the ambivalence of progress.

If we could have the wharf for the fishermen, so that they could

186

be independent of the tides, I pondered. . . . But then, I imagined next, had we any right to be independent of the tides? Dared we be? But the thing that chiefly worried me was the thought that I might be looking upon the impending death of the dory. Suppose men no longer knew how to row a boat . . . ? Should this happen, some magic would go from life.

Meanwhile, the dredger had nearly finished. One more day and that gaudily illumined calliope would have left us. We had even grown accustomed to it over that week. The beach was going to seem very desolate; it would be almost abruptly more desolate than that first moment after Labor Day when we always breathed a sigh of relief and declared ourselves delighted with the vision of the deserted sands.

Up against the wharf had been heaped enormous banks of rocks. I felt cheated, for I had not seen them being brought along. And I had supposed I had left nothing unnoticed. The sand was piled up in front of Jesse Medeiros' place, giving him now about twenty feet more land than before.

But I felt I had lost my way. A strange thing had happened. One week earlier this change had not started. The shore line was as I had always known it—each rock and breakwater and curve of sand. I could have described it to anyone, were I to have gone to the ends of the earth. This new shaping and forming of the land and sea had forced its way into my mind. I saw before me the future. I saw the growth of Wellfleet once again as a fishing town, proud of its integrity, and tossing its head at seasonal vacationists. Boats anchored against the dock, with their harvest of quahogs and scallops and clams. They had begun to take possession even while the dock was still being built. Everything was good.

But I realized with a shock that already I had forgotten what it had looked like before all this happened.

The Beach

When we think of the beach on Cape Cod, we mean the vast expanse of the back shore—the back side, as they call it here—facing the Atlantic. The gentler side, nestled in the curve of the arm of the Cape, is never the beach; it is always the bay. And, though both are built of sand and both are subject to the rhythm of the tides, yet they are utterly different. Even the life upon their shores is different; horseshoe crabs and scallops, oysters and clams cannot be found along the Atlantic at low water; they require the shelter of the bay.

This, fringing the Atlantic, is an austere, wild world. Over a large part of the year it is a lonely world, visited only by the little animals and the birds. Deer can be seen here, and skunks, and the tern nests upon the ground. Deserted sands border an empty sea.

"I remember, just as far back as 1916, how there would be fifty to sixty vessels a day, out there on the back side, passing along on the horizon," says Charlie Mayo. "There was no Canal, then, to take them the other way. We used to see so many towboats and barges, all the year round. It's kind of forlorn today. I can scarcely stand going there, it's so lonesome."

But nobody could say that it is lonesome during the months of the summer. Looking at it then, with its golden sands and the smooth blue of the ocean—the sands dotted with bright, striped umbrellas and sun-tanned, happy swimmers—looking upon this serene scene it is not easy to think of it as anything other than a mighty playground. Little family groups sit there, soaking up the sun, over the hours of daylight. They appear inviolate in their separation from the rest of the world, so that the beach is covered with self-contained, insulated clumps.

Something seems to happen to people on a beach. It may be the outcome of primitive fear; an unconscious defense against this elemental setting. Nowhere else does it happen with such fierce intensity. These secure little groups are ringed around by an invisible cordon.

"Touch us not," they seem to be saying. "We do not need you. We are off by ourselves. We are complete."

I strayed once into one of these little groups. It was at dusk, and they were eating a picnic supper. The flames from the driftwood fire danced upon their faces and played around their figures, tossing rich, abundant shadows behind them. Perhaps it was the quality of these shadows that gave me the courage to approach them on my solitary walk. After all, they *were* my friends; they could not but welcome me. And so I dared to join them. I sat with them, increasingly aware that I was an outsider, and almost hating this great ocean that did something to my friends.

Just as I was wondering how to withdraw from this gathering, the Atlantic Ocean itself came to my help. Suddenly—and with no warning whatsoever—one gigantic wave rushed up the beach, to the foot of the dunes, and swamped the picnic. While the little group was trying to rescue rugs and bottles and food, I found myself filled with benign malice and delight. The sea had asserted itself. It was supreme, though it might lie there on this summer night so treacherously calm.

This, perhaps, is why they huddle together so much, on the back shore, fused into one small entity.

"Let's go down to the beach," everyone says all summer long. But it is the visitors who say this. Not often do you see the real Cape Codders here. They know too much about this mighty mass of water and carry within them unwilling memories. Sometimes, after the summer people have left, they will go—especially at the height of a storm. But they hold a strange proprietory respect for this Atlantic and are reluctant to share it with outsiders.

And it is little wonder that they feel this, for in their blood, and in the blood of their ancestors, lies tribute to the vagaries of this sea.

One day in late October I took a neighbor with me to watch a particularly wild tide. It was a high course tide, a forced one, urged upwards by a violent northeaster, so that it must have been, at the very least, fourteen feet. She was a gentle creature and recently widowed, and I feared lest she might not really want to go to the back shore in this fury of wind and rain. As we stood on the top of the dunes, watching the churning sea that undercut the cliffs and tossed the sand high into the air, I looked round at her, wondering what she was thinking and feeling.

"It's a mighty force, water is," she said quietly. "You can quench fire, but nothing on this earth can stop the force of water."

"I know something about it," she went on, her voice scarcely audible above the thump of the breakers. "My father was lost right out there. He was a sea captain."

A sense of shame covered me, and a feeling of humility. The woman grew suddenly ennobled before me as I thought of what was contained in those few words, so quietly spoken.

This made me think of the company of ghosts that must walk the beach, stepping with bewilderment around the sun bathers and the striped umbrellas.

There would be the earliest of the Indians, back in the unknown, the men whose bones have crumbled to become the sand itself. And then the Pilgrims, watching later tribes of Indians, peeping at them in apprehension and fear. The names of our beaches testify to this: First Encounter Beach, in Eastham, and Corn Hill, in Truro, where the Pilgrims were saved from starvation by finding a cache of Indian corn. These, walking their ghostly paths along the sand, might come across an occasional Dutch phantom, strayed from the early seventeenth-century trading post on Great Island. But most certainly they would meet the mighty company of the shipwrecked, ghosts tortured by the fury of the sea, frozen ghosts who had clung to the masts of sinking ships in the middle of winter, ghosts of mothers and children, sailing the high seas with their men. They might also meet the unhappy, haunted ghosts of wreckers who had plundered the grounded vessels.

It would be a worthy gathering of the departed, walking the Great Beach; this twenty or more miles of unbroken coastline, with nothing between the tide line and the shores of Spain; this multicolored beach of ivory and rust and gold; this beach that is in obedience to the ocean, changing its form with the swing of the seasons, so that at one moment you walk along a wide stretch of sand, and then, within the space of a few months, find that the contour of the beach has been tossed into disorder beneath the

192

force of a few storms, till there is no longer this stretch of sand, but only a narrow lane at low tide between the ocean and the foot of the dune.

Walking this beach they would know, with the supersensitive awareness of the disembodied, exactly where the ribs of ships lay buried beneath the sand and comprehend the sudden appearance upon the surface of this sand of the vertebra of a whale, disclosed by the violence of a northeaster.

But most of all, I like to think, they would have felt fellowship with the men who used to walk the beach on the watch patrol, keeping them company upon their desolate dark journeys.

They must have held a sensitive knowledge of the beach, these patrolmen who were trained to live through their ears, rather than their eyes; these men so attuned to solitude that they grew to hear the slightest sound of nature around them, knowing when a hop-toad moved across their path in the black darkness, or when a tern, nesting in the sand upon the dunes, stirred upon her eggs.

The watch patrol of the Life Saving Service was four and a half miles, each way, out from Cahoon's Hollow.

A nine-mile walk is not too bad if the weather is clement and you are not spoiled yet by the age of the automobile. But it is no easy stroll.

Halfway along the beach, between the stations, there were watchhouses. But it was dark—the kind of darkness that you could not describe.

" 'And how can you tell, Captain,' " my patrolman friend George Higgins was recounting to me, " 'How can you tell, Captain,' I said to him, 'that you've reached the watchhouse? In the darkness, with nothing but darkness around you and before you and behind you, how can you tell when you've reached there?'

"The Captain knew I was young at the job, and so he wasn't

too hard on me. He was a good man, he was, and understood.

" 'Walk till you're so tired you just can't go on,' he said. 'At that spot and at that moment, you'll know you're halfway there. And then you just time yourself, from then on.' "

George Higgins was telling me of his years in the Life Saving Service.

"We had to walk that shore regularly, those days," he went on, "for if there was a vessel on the beach we had to be there, to know about it. You'd know if it was there, by sound rather than sight. You'd listen and you'd hear it above the storm. You'd hear the sail slatting, and the twisting and thumping of the timber and rigging above the storm itself. . . . You had to walk along the top of the sand dunes, for the sea ran up to the foot of the dunes. And you carried three Coston signals, just in case two of them were duds. You carried these signals and a wooden holder. And then, if you should happen to hear a vessel in distress, you put the Coston signal in the holder and twisted it into it, and lighted it. And then you knew you were perceived."

"But did you never meet a fellow patrolman?" I asked him, thinking of the utter loneliness of that life.

"No," he answered. "That is, not unless it happened to be in the daytime on a foggy day. For we had to walk the beach whenever there was a fog. But fog is nothing when it comes to darkness. After a time you can actually manage to see in the dark. But it's not just that. You know the direction in which you're going, by the wind on the side of your face. . . . Not but what we didn't get close calls, as you might say. I remember one night."

He paused, relighting his cigarette that had gone out.

"Yes?" I said. "What happened?"

"It was down there towards Monomoy Point," he went on. "The spit cut through, that night. It's a bad part, that is. There was a wicked storm—a real northeast gale, with snow. The beach was hard. And I had the two-to-four-in-the-morning watch, south. I knew the sea was breaking its shores, but I didn't know how much.

I kept on keeping that wind on the side of my face as I walked the patrol. And then I found I was getting into water, and deeper water."

Once again he stopped, and for a while I feared he was so lost in thought that he would forget he was talking to anyone. But I believe he was just reliving the horror of that night, for he went on:

"Yes, deeper and deeper in water. Foolishly I turned round. I should never have done that. And it was then I lost my bearings. Both my boots—high up my thighs—were full of water. But I kept agoing, till the water was up to my waist. And then I knew I'd really lost my bearings, for the wind was hitting me all round and I couldn't tell where I was or in what direction I was going.

And it was then I nearly got panicky, but not quite. . . . The trouble was there was snow everywhere on the ground, even on the beach, and snow, as you know, changes the look of everything. I couldn't see the watchhouse and I didn't know where I was. But then I saw the imprint of a foot. It was frozen—frozen in ice and snow upon the sand. And I followed it and it led to the watchhouse. The watchhouse was filled with snow. You could scarcely make it out, it was so filled. . . . My lantern blew out, but I managed to light it again inside the watchhouse. And I managed, too, to telephone through to Cahoon's to tell them where I was and what had happened. . . . I was soaked through, for the freezing water had been so high it had got right up to my waist, way up above my boots."

He was speaking slowly, with long pauses, as he kept pace with his recollections.

" 'What shall I do?' I asked them. 'The sea has broken its shore and is high around the spit. I'm here, but shall I stay here?' I listened for the Captain's voice, over the telephone. . . . It came small, just above the roar of the wind. And then—he was a man who truly knew what one should do, and I trusted him—he said I'd better try to make it back to the station, for if I were soaked like this the chances were I'd get frozen to death before dawn. . . . The tide has turned, as I go back, and it isn't so bad. . . . But you can get into messes, on this patrol watch, I tell you."

Unconsciously he changed from the past tense to the present, so vividly was he reliving that night.

"But how did you manage to keep to the cliffs, in the dark?" I asked him. "For, when the tide was high, you couldn't walk the beach itself."

"Oh," he said. "That's easy. You can know that you are keeping near to the edge—where you ought to be—by the way there's no

196

wind. It's a funny thing, but you just don't get the force of the wind when you walk along the extremest edge. It's as though the wind rushes up the steep side of the dunes, and rises high above you. That's the best way to know where you are walking, when it's all dark and you can easily stray from your set path. When you feel the wind you know you must get back to the edge."

And then he went all silent. In his mind he had returned to safety. But first he added:

"It was tough. God, it was tough. And you never catch me going to the back shore these days, if I can possibly help it."

That's it, I thought. That's why they leave it to the summer people who know this beach only when it is smiling and gay.

But let us forget the past, for a little while, and enjoy the beach, walking along this ever-changing, lacy-edged tide line in the space between high-water mark and low. The tide line is fringed with sea wrack: golden seaweed, deep brown seaweed, long switches of seaweed, like the tufted tails of some unknown animals; little shells, broken shells, shells of many kinds; pebbles bright-colored from the water. But there is something else to be found along this tide line. Here lie the delicate filigrees of bleached fish bones, these white, Gothic-like, intricate patternings of such beauty. What fish do they come from? And how long did it take the sun and the salt water to bleach them to this purity? You question, and all you know is that they lie here, on the sand, some of the most exquisite of nature's designs.

Looking at them I find myself singing the verse of an old Cape Cod song:

> Cape Cod girls
> They have no combs.
> They comb their hair
> With codfish bones.

And I remember, too, the bleaching bones of a blackfish I found in the cove.

It was really my six-year-old friend Robbie who found them. "Be quiet and listen," he whispered, slinking up to me with his secret. "I've found a dolphin—yes, a real dolphin. And you'd better come along with me this very minute before anyone else discovers it."

There is enchantment in the word "dolphin," calling up images from a mythological world of fantasy. I saw dolphins leaping in the Mediterranean, in the Adriatic, off the isles of Greece. Robbie did not know what he had done for me.

Together we crept to the edge of the cove where, among the beach grasses, we found a stranded blackfish. It must have been washed in on a floodtide a very long time back, for there was no meat left on it and not too much smell. The bones were exposed; the teeth shone in their whiteness, under the summer sun.

"Isn't it lovely," murmured the child. "Lovely, lovely, lovely."

Carefully we examined the bones: the long delicate ribs, the wing-shaped shoulder blade, the breast bone with part of the clavicle still adhering to it.

"If that were painted gold," sighed Robbie, "yes, if only that were gilt, it would look exactly like part of Queen Elizabeth's crown, or part of her golden coach."

The child had sensed the beauty in these bones.

We brought the breast bone back with us—it and the wing-shaped scapula and a few of the ribs and the cleanest of the vertebrae. I cherished them with a special vehemence.

This vehemence was due to a fantastic happening of many years ago. On one of my walks on the beach I had suddenly come across a perfect specimen of an enormous whale vertebra. It lay there embedded in the sand, close to a shuttered shack, belonging, I feared, to the absent occupants of this shack. Never have I had a worse struggle with my conscience. I wanted to steal that whale bone. And so I hurriedly left, resisting temptation. Next day, drawn irresistibly to the scene, I returned. But I found no vertebra. Had it been a dream, I wondered?

The strange coincidence is that, several years later, when I

visited a friend in Connecticut, who summers on the Cape, I saw this whale bone in her living room. Envy and frustration overwhelmed me, as I realized what had happened.

Now, I told myself, this time I would be sure of my "dolphin's" breast bone.

Unfortunately the bones still smelt too much to keep them in the house. I put them out in the yard, for sun and rain to purify. And then, one morning, the precious breast bone had vanished.

"The whale vertebra," I reminded myself. "My friend who loves bones. I believe she is here on the Cape just now."

I put a poignant notice of my loss on the town bulletin-board, assuring the pilferer that all would be forgiven, and suggesting an anonymous, nocturnal return of the breast bone. But it never came back. And then one day Robbie ran to me in tears:

"I've found out what happened," he howled. "I saw our dog Goldie trying to take away the dolphin's shoulder blade. It was her who took our breast bone. She's got a sudden craze for burying bones."

We never did recover the beautiful thing.

But with the normal acquisitiveness of those who walk the beach —that acquisitiveness which even a moralist like Thoreau was finding hard to resist—an acquisitiveness that would brand one as a thief, anywhere other than in that narrow strip of sand, between high tide and low, I, too, search upon the shore for what I can find. After a three-day northeaster I am as rapacious as anyone. I haul great logs and branches of beautiful silvered driftwood along the beach and pack them in the back of my car. (Once I brought an enormous root of a tree back with me, all the way from the tip of Cape Breton. But that was not for burning; it stands, now, on a Connecticut hillside in its smooth silver beauty, reminding me always of the far North.)

As the driftwood burns in the fireplace, tossing the strangest blues and greens into the yellow flames, it brings the magic of the unknown. This hunk of wood, satin-smooth and bleached by the ocean, stained brown in places from the rust of nails: where did it come from? Was it part of a ship, wrecked up the coast? Or a tree, uprooted in a storm? Conjecture brings an element of romance to the fire burning in the grate.

But this element of romance is not all, for the essence of the beachcomber lies even deeper. It satisfies, I believe, the privileged lawlessness of mankind. The sand of the beach carries upon its surface objects tossed up by the sea, from hundreds of miles away, belonging to nobody on this earth. And why, then, should we not

200

grab them? Sister at heart at all wreckers, I grab with the rest.

I will confess. As one of my most precious possessions I treasure two hand-carved, wooden decoy ducks. They were given to me as a most appropriately timed gift from chance, one Christmas morning, on the shore line near Great Island. Did I question for a moment as to whether or not I should take them? No. My head held high, my booty hidden as much as possible beneath my thick winter coat, I strode back to the car, exultant. And the two black, wooden decoy ducks stand sentinel, to this day, against my fireplace. Perhaps I have no right to be somewhat wrathful, still, about that whale vertebra?

So long as the tide line will give us shells we are all right. Then, in entire honesty, we can satisfy this crazy urge. For which of us has not collected shells? Early each year indiscriminatingly we start. And then, as the summer passes, we grow progressively selective, till the inevitable moment comes when we look at our greedy amassings and decide to toss them away. Out go the slightly imperfect scallop shells, the big whelk with a flaw, the little fairy boats in which we had so deeply delighted. And why do we do this? And what do we leave? A gap, and a need, awaiting fulfillment next year.

But we have few shells, up here on Cape Cod. I say this as I fling my mind back to the years I spent in the South. There, along the shores of the Carolinas, on those sands that are silver, rather than golden, you could not avoid treading upon shells, there were so many. The sand was covered with the fragile hinged tellens, colored like subtle rainbows. The beaches were blossoming sea meadows.

And then, traitor, still, to the Cape, I think of the little pools of Maine, where the water stays behind at low tide, imprisoned in the hollows of rocks. There, within the boundaries of a few rocks, you can see in microcosm the whole world of color and shapes.

But this treachery does not stay with me for long. I remember, suddenly, the great expanse of sand, upon the back shore, and the feeling of calm space. I see it at night, in the summer, at the height of a heat wave, with an orange moon rising over the sea and the offshore wind bringing a sickly sweet land-scent, a mixture of pines and sweet fern, that overpowers any scent from the sea. The tide is very low, and you can wade out towards the path of the moon that is bronzing the water, feeling, rather than perceiving, the edge of the ocean. You can wade across to the sand bars, and even the guzzles reach only up the thigh. It is a gentle, benign sea, on such a night. And I remember other nights, at the full of the moon, with the scattering flurry of sandpipers before me, as I walk the edge of the ocean. Again this ocean holds no hint of danger.

And I know that this beauty of gentle calmness is every bit as much a part of our back shore as are the furies of winter. So, too, is the summer sunrise over this sea, bursting upon the sand dunes in a splendor of sudden gold.

But I believe there is something else about the beach that comforts and delights us. More than pleasure in the beauty of sand— sand ribbed and patterned by the lapping and pounding of the water, sand covered with the tell-tale marks of the feet of the birds, or the flurry swept by the tips of their feathers; more even than pleasure in the ocean itself, there is the awareness of the rhythm of the tides.

For we have need of this rhythm. Watching the discipline of the tides, with their evident rhythm, we can surrender our fears, reminded that we are part of the universe and live within the pattern of an order that is beyond our control. The fisherman is aware of this. Working with the swing of the tides that he cannot avoid and is unable to ignore, he carries within him a deep, wise patience that nothing can destroy. From him we can learn.

202